A STRANGER IN THE FOG

KU-033-556

• SILVER LINK RAILWAY ANTHOLOGIES •

A STRANGER IN THE FOG

and other chilling tales from the tracks

• Barry Herbert •

• CHILLERS, THRILLERS AND ECCENTRICS •

from

The NOSTALGIA *Collection*

To my Mother
whose support was so vital

A Silver Link book
from
The NOSTALGIA *Collection*

© W. Barry Herbert 1989 and 2001

All rights reserved. No part of this publication may be reproduced, stored in a retrieval system or transmitted, in any form or by any means, electronic, mechanical, photocopying, recording or otherwise, without prior permission in writing from Silver Link Publishing Ltd.

First published as *Railway Ghosts and Phantoms* by David & Charles in 1989
This edition first published 2001

British Library Cataloguing in Publication Data

ISBN 1 85794 152 7

Silver Link Publishing Ltd
The Trundle
Ringstead Road
Great Addington
Kettering
Northants NN14 4BW

Tel/Fax: 01536 330588
email: sales@nostalgiacollection.com
Website: www.nostalgiacollection.com

Printed and bound in Great Britain

Contents

Acknowledgements   7

1 Bridge 173   9
2 The barman's story – a sequel to 'Bridge 173'   12
3 The old loco shed   14
4 Glasgow underground hauntings   18
5 The mystery children of Charfield   21
6 Blea Moor Tunnel   24
7 The Balcombe Tunnel ghosts   26
8 Ingrow Tunnel   28
9 Box Tunnel   29
10 Echoes of the Tay Bridge disaster   30
11 Lincolnshire signal box mysteries   31
12 The little old guard   39
13 Tulse Hill station   40
14 The broken-hearted lover   41
15 The suicidal student   44
16 Footsteps in the ballast   47
17 The mystery lights   49
18 The haunted recording studio   50
19 Last across   52
20 Dicky o'Tunstead   54
21 The Luck of Edenhall   56
22 The spectral train of Kyle   58
23 French Drove & Gedney Hill   59
24 Heard but not seen   62

25   Second sight?   64
26   The train in the night   67
27   A stranger in the fog   69
28   The visitor   72
29   Ghosts at Kidlington   74
30   Gas lamps and ghosts   77
31   The man in the mist   79
32   The man in the black beret   82
33   The revenge of the old soldier   84
34   The sealed tunnel   86
35   The wreck of the Scottish Mail   88
36   The Hexthorpe ghost   91
37   The letter   93
38   Sharpthorne Tunnel   96
39   The sinister suitcase   99
40   The mystery of the sad lady   102
41   The Midland brake-van   106
42   The phantom 'Western'   111
43   'Runaway trucks!'   113
44   Footsteps on platform 4   115
45   Hibaldstow Crossing   117
46   The ghost of Fair Becca   119
47   Strange happenings at Webb House   121
48   My old friend   124
49   The return of Binns Bankcroft   126

Acknowledgements

*M*y grateful thanks are due to all those who helped me, in many ways, to compile the material for this book. I would particularly like to thank: E. L. Anderson, Stuart Bailey, Mrs C. Barker, R. J. Barry, R. L. P. Belanger, James Blake, Mr P. Briggs, H. B. Brookes, H. Bunting, H. E. Caunt, P. S. Chapman, Collins Publishers, Mr G. Coverdale, P. Craddock, Derek Cross, John Daubney, A. Dixon, A. Dodsworth, D. Duke, Durham County Library, B. C. Essex, Mrs E. Fox, Peter Grant, Andrew Green (Fontana Books), J. Hallam, B. Hamilton, Peter Handford, Jack Hayden, Mr G. Heathcliffe, M. A. Houghton, Ted Hudson, P. Hussellbury, H. C. Johnston, Doris Jones-Baker, G. Knight, G. Leslie, J. J. Leslie, A. J. Ludlam, Tom McDevitte, John McDonald, I. McGill, J. McIlmurray, Rev D. K. McKenzie, J. Marshall, Nick Matthews, R. R. Mester, G. Nash, *The Observer* newspaper, The Oxford Mail Newspaper Ltd, Patrick Stephens Limited, PC 1405, Mr D. Pearson, E. W. Poulter, M. Pritchett, Peter Richardson, Mr R. Robinson (who gave legal advice when necessary), D. M. Ross, John Rothera, P. Screeton, C. Selway, E. A. Shaw, M. Squires, James Tomlinson, Peter Underwood (Fontana/Collins Books), David Walker, D. Walker and D. Reynolds, C. E. Whitehead, L. A. Whitehouse, B. J. Willey, D. Winn, Simon Winser, A. Withnall, R. J. Woodward, and all other sources of help, direct and indirect.

Thanks are also due to my friends and everyone else who gave advice and encouragement.

1
Bridge 173

*B*ridge 173 was an agricultural occupation bridge spanning a deep railway cutting, and was used by the local farmer to give access to two large lineside fields. It was a very sound brick structure built in about 1868, but it had a notorious reputation for being a 'Lover's Leap', no doubt due to the fact that several suicide attempts had been made from its high parapet, most of them successful.

One particular night, young John Armitage, a very junior passed engine cleaner with no notion of the bridge's notoriety, was firing a goods train with his mate, driver Sam Webster. He had just fired round and sat down to rest. Sam gave him a smile of approval and said, 'Good lad, young John, now put your injector on, shut it off when you've got nearly a full "glass", then have a few minutes. I'll tell you when to fire up again just before we go up the bank.'

Young John did as he was told. This was his first main-line trip and he was grateful to Sam for taking him and for his advice. The shed running foreman had asked Sam if he would take the youngster as there was no one else available at the time. He had explained that although the lad had not been on the main line before, he was good, reliable and sensible. Sam had agreed without any hesitation, knowing that to wait for the first available fireman would delay his train's departure.

John had been delighted. He had done some pilot work, firing for some of the older shunt link drivers, and had also fired on the local 'pick-up' goods, but this at last was the real thing.

So far, driver Sam Webster was pleased with his young mate's performance and had noted with approval how he used his firing shovel to spread the coal systematically round the firebox and how he was able to fire through the firehole door trap without having to open the door itself. With a little bit more experience and confidence, he would undoubtedly make a 'good 'un'.

Young John, seated on his cabside fireman's seat, looked interestedly about him. Poking his head out from the cab, to get a little cooling draught, he noticed that they were about to enter a long deep cutting and marvelled at the way that it had been cut through almost solid rock. The track took a right-hand curve and for the first time he saw the bridge standing high above it.

But as they approached the bridge he had a shock. Although it was almost dusk, he was certain that he had seen someone or something fall from the bridge. Momentarily frozen with shock, he recovered his scattered wits and shouted, 'Sam, stop – someone's jumped off the bridge.'

Sam acted quickly. As a main-line driver, his reflexes were excellent. Smartly closing the regulator, he made a partial application of the steam brake, paused, released it, paused once again, then, when he heard the wagon buffers come together, made a full brake application. He knew of course that he would never be able to halt the train before it reached the bridge and he had the safety of his guard, Gerry Briggs, to think about. If he had made a full brake application, Gerry would have been thrown from one end of his brake-van to the other, with possible injury.

As the train slowed down, Sam came over to the fireman's side and looked out. Seeing nothing, he suddenly remembered the legend of the bridge. He looked at young John, now white and shaking with the shock. 'Don't worry, young John,' he said, to comfort and reassure him. 'You kept a good look-out.'

As the train slowed to a halt, he remembered the other drivers, mostly 'old hands', who had talked about Bridge 173, and how some of them had joked about the 'strange sightings' near it.

They had stopped about a train's length beyond the bridge. 'Stop on the engine, John,' said Sam. 'I'll go back and have a look and see the guard.'

Walking back to the end of the train, he found Gerry standing on the track beside his brake-van.

'What's up then, Sam?' asked Gerry. 'Anything wrong with the engine?'

'No. My mate thought he saw something or someone fall off the bridge.'

The guard climbed up into his brake-van to collect a can of detonators in case he had to protect the train. 'Come on then, Sam, let's have a look.'

Reaching the bridge, they had a good look round but found nothing.

'Bloody bridge,' Gerry said. 'The last time this happened was about five years ago, when Jack Thompson saw something. Do you remember everybody laughed about it? Come on, Sam, let's get going. If we get a move on, we'll make the time up. I don't think we should report it, do you?'

'Not so likely,' Sam agreed. 'I'll tell young John not to say anything.'

Once on the move again, Sam told his young fireman all about the legend of the bridge. 'Will you have to report it?' John asked.

'Not so bloody likely,' Sam said. 'If I tell anyone that we stopped to look for a ghost, they'll laugh at me, and if I was you I wouldn't tell your mates either. Just tell them that you now know where Bridge 173 is.'

2
The barman's story – a sequel to 'Bridge 173'

One sunny autumn afternoon in 1963 John and Mary, a couple on holiday in the West Country, were walking along a disused trackbed with their two Jack Russell terriers, Tina and Spot, who were enjoying their walk as much as their owners. There was so much to sniff at and they had already found two rabbits and set up a flock of partridges.

When they reached the approach to what appeared to be a long deep cutting, Mary stopped. 'Let's go back – I think we've gone far enough and it looks dark and spooky.' Was it a woman's intuition?

However, the two dogs settled the matter, racing on ahead. John looked at his watch.

'Come on, Mary, we can go on for another ten minutes, and I'd like to find out what's around that bend.'

So reluctantly she followed her husband through the cutting. Eventually they saw ahead of them a bridge standing high and spanning the cutting, its red, crumbling brickwork now seldom used by anyone. As they drew nearer John could just make out a plate bearing the number 173.

Suddenly the dogs, who were sniffing this exciting new country, stopped. Ears pricked, hair rising on their necks, they backed slowly towards John and Mary, then they howled, turned and ran back through the cutting, leaving their owners puzzled and frightened.

Mary shuddered. 'I don't like this place – it seems sad and depressing. Don't you think it's turned cold?'

John had to agree – he too felt a bit uneasy and scared, but didn't want to show his fear to Mary. 'OK, let's go back to the hotel, then we'll have a nice cup of tea.' Mary smiled and kissed him.

Later that evening, when they were seated comfortably in the bar, Mary brought up the subject of the eerie feeling in the cutting; they agreed that it had been a most disturbing experience and that there must be some explanation. As he ordered their drinks, John asked Steve the barman if he knew anything about it.

'Bridge 173, sir?' replied Steve. 'It's haunted, and I would keep well away from it. It's bad news around here, sir – it seems to attract suicides. They used to come here, yes, to this hotel to spend their last nights before they went to that bridge to hurl themselves off, sometimes in front of a train; but now that the line has gone and the track removed we don't get so many coming to end their days. Now only Alf Hurst – he farms the land either side of the cutting – uses it to get across, but even he doesn't like it. The wind always blows cold in that cutting and across the old bridge.'

John listened, fascinated by Steve's story. 'Mary and I took our dogs down there this afternoon and I must admit we didn't like it. Mary was quite frightened. We won't go again, I can assure you.'

Steve nodded. 'Very wise, sir. They used to call the spot under the bridge "Lover's Leap". It's a brooding, desolate place, that.'

Mary joined them at the bar, and the two men stopped talking and smiled at her.

'Can I have my drink? It seems as if you two will talk all night,' she said. 'Let's go and sit down, dear.' She took John's arm.

'Just a minute, sir,' said Steve. Mary returned to their table as Steve whispered to John. 'One thing that might interest you – last year our manager jumped from that bridge and broke his neck . . .'

3
The old loco shed

*T*he following story was told to me by a retired engine driver, who revisited his father's old depot some years after its closure.

'The old loco shed stood gaunt, derelict and roofless amidst the mounds of brick rubble and refuse surrounding it. The once busy building, now with the skeletal, unclad girders of its roof standing stark against the darkening sky, was just a ghost of its former self. As it was soon to be demolished I was taking the opportunity of looking round to see if I could find anything of interest relating to it to add to my growing collection of "railwayana".

The loco shed had many sentimental memories for me as my late father had been a main-line driver there many years ago before the branch line, with its four stations, marshalling sidings, loco shed and workshops, closed shortly after the closure of the two adjacent collieries. The branch line had survived for a few years as a single line until its final demise.

As I passed what had been the marshalling yard and sidings, I glanced at the rows of rusting buffer stops and rotting wooden buffer beams, and conjured up a picture of the lines of laden coal wagons waiting to be dispatched and the coal empties waiting to be taken to the collieries to be filled. It was a typically cold, wet, late autumnal afternoon as I walked along the old trackbed, avoiding the many puddles of murky rainwater on my way. I stopped momentarily to look at the old "cenotaph", or what remained of it.

The once modern coaling plant was now just a mass of huge broken lumps of concrete. Would there be anything collectable there, I wondered. I decided against looking into the tumbledown wooden hut that had once housed the coal hopper controls – the rotting wooden walkway looked too perilous to risk injury – so I continued on my way to the shed, now some 70 or 80 yards away.

I stopped about 20 yards from the shed, appalled at the scene of utter desolation and neglect. One of the shed's huge, wooden doors, the only survivor, hung crazily on one rusting hinge, swaying slightly in the stiffening breeze. Continuing on my way, I saw that the outer and inner ash pits were filled with rubble and rubbish of every kind. What an inglorious end to what had once been a busy loco shed, and the scene of so much activity in its heyday.

Reaching the shed, I stepped over several mounds of brick and other rubble and went inside, searching the wet streaked brick walls for anything that could be identifed with the depot. One of the rusting iron pipes fastened to the wall, and apparently coming from what remained of the old boilerhouse inside, had a plate fixed to it, near the stump of what must have been a water stop valve. It could be of interest, so, taking a piece of cotton waste out of my pocket, I cleaned off the accumulated filth only to discover that on it was stamped "ON-OFF". It was brass, so I decided that it was collectable; it was one souvenir at least, and although not identifiable with the shed, at least I knew where it had come from.

Walking further into the shed, I paused and looked around, wondering how many times my father must have walked through it. Then, on an impulse, I retraced my steps, following the run of the old water wash-out pipes until I found myself in the remains of what must have been the old boilerhouse. It was there that I made my really good find. I saw a corner of a rusted iron plate protruding from a pile of bricks, and eagerly set about freeing it from its rubble prison. It took me about three or four minutes to rescue it, then I looked at my "prize". Cleaning off the muck I was delighted to discover that it read "LNWR-BOILERHOUSE-PRIVATE", and must have come from the boilerhouse door. It was not too big or cumbersome to take away, so I packed it in my stout old haversack and returned to the shed.

It was getting dark now, the wind had freshened, and the rain was gusting through the length of the shed, so I decided that it was time to pack up and head for the nearest hospitable pub where I had been told I would be able to get a good meal of hot pie and peas. Dad had often spoken about the Railway Hotel just across the road from what remained of the station, and how he had played the battered old piano for a sing-song with his pals. Perhaps I would be able to conjure up his image while indulging myself with my meal and drink.

On my way out of the shed, I suddenly realised that I was not on my own. There, walking down the middle of the shed in the gloom, I espied a dark, blue-clad figure apparently wearing what Dad used to call a "steam-raiser", a shiny-topped peaked cap. The figure walked slowly down the shed. I was not surprised to be unable to see his face as it was getting dark, and I was just about to speak when suddenly, abruptly, the figure disappeared. Had it been a figment of imagination, brought about by the increasing gloom, and the aura of the surrounding dereliction? No, I knew that I had seen someone, or something.

I had never believed in ghosts, but what I had seen was unaccountable. Suddenly I heard a loud crash near me, scaring me out of my wits. The old shed door had crashed to the floor, and would swing no more. That was enough for me, the last straw. I had seen and heard enough. Already startled by the apparition, the crashing down of the big heavy door completely unnerved me.

I ran out of the shed, not looking back, raced across the old marshalling yard, out of the tumbledown gateway of the station, across the road and into the brightly lit warmth of the Railway Hotel bar. Faces looked up at me as I burst abruptly into the bar room. One old chap said, "What's up lad, tha' looks as if tha's seen a ghost!"

After getting my breath, I said, "I think I have."

One kindly old chap stood up and said, "Come on mate, sit down here, I'll get you a pint then you can tell us your story."

As I sat down, another old boy seated next to me said, "Have you been walking on the old trackbed then?"

"Yes," I replied.

Another said, "I bet you've been into the loco shed."

"Yes," I said. "How did you know?"

"Tha's not first one to get a shock there, mate," he answered. "What did you see then?"

I told them about the apparition, how I had seen someone walking down the shed, then suddenly disappearing. The kindly old chap who had given up his seat for me brought me my pint, saying, "Drink this, mate – you'll feel better when tha's supped that."

While I gratefully sipped my pint they told me the story. When the branch line and the loco shed was working, one driver had unfortunately failed the railway doctor's examination with defective colour vision and as a result had been relegated to fire-lighting and steam-raising duties. He used to come in here regularly for a pint, they said.

"I was only a young chap at the time," said one, "but I remember him well. Fred Grisenthwaite were his name. He were never the same when he came off main line. It was a pity too about his accident, as if he hadn't had enough bad luck."

"What happened then?" I asked.

"He were firin' up and steamin' an engine when it happened. A tube burst and the blow-back threw him against the tender end. He must have hit his head for it killed him. At the time we said, 'Poor old Fred, we'll never see him again.' We haven't, but others have, including you now, evidently."

I had by now recovered my scattered senses, and after finishing off an enjoyable meal of pie and peas and my second pint, I thanked my friends and left the hospitable bar. It had without doubt been a day to remember, and now, whenever I look at my LNWR boilerhouse plate, I think of poor unfortunate Fred Grisenthwaite and his tragic demise, and recall the Railway Hotel bar room and the kind friends I met that night.'

4
Glasgow underground hauntings

The Glasgow underground railway system has, like its London counterpart, witnessed some very strange and totally unexplained events. Sceptics will scoff as usual, but my informants are adamant in the truth of their accounts.

The Glasgow system serves a vital transport function, running in a circle beneath the city centre. A number of strange, ghostly occurrences are recorded in the book *I Belong to Glasgow* by Bill Hamilton and Gordon Carsely, to whom I am most obliged for the following information.

In the old days, before the system closed for extensive modernisation, there was no physical access from the running lines to Govan car sheds and workshops, so when stock was brought out of the tunnels for repair and maintenance, the vehicles had to be lifted bodily off the track by means of a large overhead crane up through pits into the workshops. At night, after the close of the service, it was the practice to stable the empty trains end to end on the running lines in the tunnels on each side of the shed car pits, the end doors of each vehicle, which permitted ready exit of passengers in the event of an emergency, opened to allow access to the lines of stabled trains for cleaners and others whose nocturnal duties took them into the subway tunnels.

On one occasion a team of five men went down into the tunnels, passing through the line of empty stabled cars. On reaching the last train they found a colleague talking to a middle-aged man dressed in a light-coloured raincoat and flat cap who was assumed to have been overcarried on the last train when it went out of service at Capland Road station. The gang led the stranger back through the empty trains to the car shed pits where he could gain access to the street. Looking back at regular intervals to see if he was following, the men eventually reached the sheds, but were astonished to find that the man had vanished. They went back and searched the trains but the stranger had indeed disappeared. They all agreed that he had been there, and that they had all seen him, so they were all completely baffled.

Govan car sheds were reputedly haunted by a figure that was seen from time to time in a driving compartment, but on investigation was found to have disappeared and was nowhere to be found; the cab was empty, yet strangely cold!

Cleaners working in the tunnels between Kelvinbridge and Hillhead stations used to report hearing disembodied voices of women singing, while an accident in 1922 is believed to be the explanation for the appearance of the 'Grey Lady' whose ghostly form has been reported in the tunnel near Shields Road station. In that year a lady and a little girl (presumably her daughter) fell from an otherwise deserted station platform into the path of an oncoming train; on seeing the incident, the station master attempted to rescue them both but was only able to save the girl.

Two maintenance gangs who were working one night some distance apart on a section of track noticed a mysterious light between them, but despite searching the area nothing could be found to explain the phenomenon.

Finally, at around 3am one Sunday in 1967, pump man Willie Baxter was detailed to go through the tunnels from St Enoch to Bridge Street station, where he was to attend to a tank located beneath the stairs. After walking for some time, covering about half the distance between the two stations, Willie became aware of a steady, rather unnerving sound just ahead of him, as if someone was hammering the rails. The ganger whose section this was, and who might therefore have been responsible, had passed through some 90 minutes earlier.

Willie Baxter was gripped by fear – he hated the dark tunnels anyway. He stopped walking, and the noise stopped. By now he was probably near the point where the tunnels passed under the

River Clyde, and it was said that it was possible to hear the sound of a ship's propeller whenever a vessel passed overhead. However, Willie was certain that this could not account for the strange noise, so he continued, only to find that the noise started again even louder. That was it! He'd had enough, so he turned and ran for his life back to St Enoch and the fresh air.

Discussing the experience with his workmates later, the reaction was divided. Some voiced complete disbelief, some agreed, as they too had had similar experiences, while others just nodded agreement with Willie.

I am told that there have been further incidents since the system re-opened following modernisation, but so far no one has supplied any details. My own belief is that tunnels are very emotive places and if one is susceptible to paranormal events they are just the sort of place for it to happen.

5

The mystery children of Charfield

The quiet Gloucestershire village of Charfield is on the former LMS main line between Gloucester and Bristol, and before closure in 1965 its local station served the surrounding community and carried a fair amount of passenger and freight traffic. However, the village hit the headlines in a tragic way just before dawn on 13 October 1928 when a terrible accident and fire occurred there.

The driver of the 10pm down LMS Leeds-Bristol passenger and mail train apparently overran a stop signal at danger and plunged into the front section of the 9.15pm Oxley Sidings to Bristol GWR fitted goods train, which was being reversed into a siding to clear a path for the express. The mail then collided with another freight passing in the opposite direction, the up 4.45am Westerleigh to Gloucester empties.

Interlocking meant that the signalman could not have cleared his down signals for the mail, yet although both footplatemen on the express admitted to not having seen the home signals on the approach to Charfield, both men were equally emphatic that they had seen the proceeding distant signal, and they said that it was showing a green light and in the clear position.

Immediately following the accident it was discovered that the repeater instrument in Charfield box bore this out, although investigation showed that the distant arm was slightly inclined due to debris from the crash bearing on the signal wire – but not sufficient to show a green light through the spectacle plate. To have shown a green light a heavier weight must have been lying across the signal wire. Or had the signal been tampered with? The footplatemen had nothing to gain by lying about the position of the distant signal when they admitted not seeing the home signals at all.

The mystery therefore remains, but it is not the only mystery attached to the Charfield disaster. Indeed, the one that most concerns us in the context of the strange and uncanny is the riddle of the unclaimed bodies.

Fifteen lives were lost in the accident and the ensuing fire, which raged for 12 hours. Two of the dead were children, a girl aged about eight or nine and a boy of about 11 years; they were travelling together, but otherwise unaccompanied. It was alleged that at first the railway company denied that they had been travelling on the train at all, and it was also suggested that they were chance victims of the holocaust and had happened to be wandering by the railway at the time. However, the evidence of the fireman who was on the footplate of the mail engine disproved the allegations, for he had seen them together on the train after it had arrived at Birmingham New Street station around 2.30am, when they had waved to him. He subsequently saw them laughing and talking with the guard before the train left Birmingham and described both youngsters as well dressed; the boy was wearing a school uniform of yellow and brown with a cap to match and a scarf. Regrettably the guard was killed in the crash.

In the aftermath of the accident the bodies of the two children were recovered from the wreckage and laid beside the track with the other victims of the tragedy, but their charred remains were beyond recognition. They were never claimed, nor was any connection established between them and the other passengers, and in consequence they were never identified.

Most of the victims were buried in the village churchyard of St James where the LMS erected a memorial with the names of those laid to rest there. The base of the memorial is inscribed with ten names and the emotive words 'Two Unknown'.

There is even doubt in some quarters as to whether the unfortunate children were in fact interred at Charfield, for it was said that an Army vehicle was noticed briefly at the scene of the accident, and it has been suggested that some of the remains, possibly those of the children, were removed amid the general confusion.

Someone, somewhere must have been concerned for and worried about these unfortunate children and found their absence odd; surely, too, someone must have paid their fare and seen them off on their journey. And was no one waiting for them at their intended destination?

6
Blea Moor Tunnel

*T*alk to many a railwayman about Blea Moor Tunnel on the famous Settle & Carlisle line and you will find either a spontaneous reaction of a flow of stories or complete and total silence. This bore has a very unpleasant reputation and the local people do not like to go near the place at night, especially as the rail traffic today has been considerably reduced.

The late railway photographer Derek Cross had been through the tunnel on the footplate of an 'A3' 'Pacific' and a Class 40 diesel, and on both occasions he had been very pleased to see the other end, such was its evil, brooding and emotive reputation.

Situated below a hill between the valleys of the Ribble and Eden, the bore marked the determination of the Midland Railway to refuse to be beaten by obstacles that could be overcome by sheer practical means. Its construction was very difficult in the Victorian age; men were killed during the excavations, and its depth of 500 feet below the surface at one point exposed numerous problems.

At the height of the Steam Age over 100 trains passed through Blea Moor Tunnel each day, and the acrid, choking fumes found their way up through the ventilators on the top of the hill. However, the tremendous build-up of soot on the tunnel roof tended to clog up the apertures of the brick ventilators, so a 'blow-back' effect was often experienced by footplate crews.

A correspondent, Mr A. W. Kewish of Barrow-in-Furness, Cumbria, tells of his experience in Blea Moor Tunnel; he wishes to state that neither he nor his wife are psychic. They were on a rail tour over several routes in the North not usually used by passenger trains, but they did not realise that they had to travel through Blea Moor Tunnel. They travelled up the goods line from Blackburn, waited for a clear road at Hellifield Junction, then travelled up the 'Long Drag' towards the summit. The coaches were six- or eight-a-side compartment vehicles with sliding-ventilator windows; it was warm in the carriage by the time the tunnel was reached, so a top-light was opened.

Neither Mr nor Mrs Kewish had any idea what was in Blea Moor Tunnel, but they were both very frightened – their one desire was to get off the train as quickly as possible! They were appalled by the sickly, overpowering, cloying sweet smell that pervaded the carriage – Mr Kewish described it as not dissimilar to incense! His wife vowed that she would never, ever travel through Blea Moor Tunnel again.

There would therefore appear to be something unknown or untold about Blea Moor Tunnel – there has been much speculation but very few facts or details. Whether deserved or not, it certainly has an evil reputation, perhaps because of its lonely location and the emotive nature of a one-and-a-half-mile hole through a hill. Perhaps one day something will come to light to explain the mysteries of Blea Moor Tunnel.

7
The Balcombe Tunnel ghosts

*T*rain-spotting had hardly become an attraction for the boys of the day when the first Easter excursion thundered through Balcombe Tunnel en route to Brighton. It was no ordinary train, but one made up of 57 carriages and hauled by no fewer than six locomotives, and it travelled the 50 miles from London in 4½ hours. No doubt as the snorting monsters emerged from the Black Hole of Balcombe in a cloud of smoke and steam, the merry crowd of villagers who watched from the top of the embankment gave a wary cheer and wondered what the world was coming to!

A hundred years later, during the Second World War, the scene at Balcombe was much the same; trains faster and far more frequent were still thundering through the tunnel, but without the cheering villagers to wave them on their way, just sentries posted at both ends. One night, early in the war, German planes droned overhead and dropped bombs along the railway line, possibly aiming to destroy the tunnel and so cut a supply link to the Channel ports and the British armies in France.

Mr E. Myer of Guestling, Sussex, well remembers the night that he was on sentry duty from midnight to 2am; several bombs fell close to the tunnel entrance and he decided to take refuge in one of the recesses let into the tunnel wall. After about 5 minutes he saw the strange sight of what he took to be three men approaching. He challenged them in the usual way, shouting 'Halt or I fire!' At this the figures became somewhat hazy, then vanished. As Mr Myer had been on duty under somewhat arduous conditions for several months he decided that his nerves were playing tricks on him and that he was having hallucinations.

However, the next day, on his next tour of duty, he met the foreman platelayer when he arrived for work. The platelayer commented on the air raid and that he never expected to see soldiers guarding the tunnel, especially the inside, for a second time, it having been guarded during the First World War. The foreman told him that three soldiers had been killed near the spot that Mr Myer had been in the recess the previous night; they had apparently been run down by a train just inside the tunnel mouth.

Today London to Brighton trains still roar through Balcombe Tunnel, the passengers completely unaware of the tragedy that will haunt the darkened bore for ever.

8
Ingrow Tunnel

*T*here are many unexplained events on the preserved
Keighley & Worth Valley line, which runs for 5 miles from
Keighley to the terminus at Oxenhope. The strange occurrence
at Ingrow Tunnel has no logical explanation, so perhaps must be
regarded as a paranormal phenomenon. Black smoke billows
from the tunnel as if emanating from a steam locomotive, which
is very possible considering that the K&WVR has plenty of
steam motive power. But on the occasions with which we are
concerned, none of the preservation society's locos were in
steam, so therefore could not be blamed for the smoke.

Two men, Supervisor D. Narey and his pal Arnold Illingworth,
say the smell of the smoke is remarkably like that of a steam
engine. They have investigated the source, and although they
have walked the tunnel they have found no explanation except
that the phenomenon seems to stop in a recess under the Halifax
Road. Another strange aspect of the mystery is that the two men
claim that the smoke came out of the tunnel mouth towards the
station, yet a breeze was blowing the other way. Mr Narey ruled
out smoke from nearby factories or bonfires in the Wesley Place
area.

Railway official Graham Mitchell says that the original tunnel
builders were plagued with problems, including part of the
nearby Wesley Chapel sliding away. 'We don't know that anyone
was killed or injured near there so there shouldn't be anyone
haunting it.'

9
Box Tunnel

Box Tunnel on the former Great Western line from Bristol to London is nearly 2 miles long, which is a lot of tunnel to maintain for any permanent way gang, whom I do not imagine relish the thought of working in the dark, damp, gloomy bore.

The tunnel was built by Isambard Kingdom Brunel and opened in 1841, and at the time was acclaimed as an engineering masterpiece. To many early rail travellers, however, the gloom of the tunnel was very frightening. They harboured irrational notions about it, as it was some 300 feet below the surface; some of the local people feared the whole land area would collapse, while fears were also expressed by some passengers that the tunnel might collapse while they were travelling through it, or that they might suffocate from the lack of air because it was so long!

In the latter days of steam, maintenance workers near or inside the tunnel were absolutely convinced that they heard the sound of an approaching train when none was due. In fact, some of them swore that they saw a phantom train roaring into or out of the tunnel. Of course the sceptics laughed at such a far-fetched tale, although others were inclined to accept the men's story.

Tunnels are strange places, and it is not difficult for the mind to conjure up thoughts of terror, such as the possibility of being run down in the dark. Certainly many gangers refused to work in, or near, Box Tunnel, such was the reputation it earned.

10
Echoes of the Tay Bridge disaster

On 28 December 1879 Sir Thomas Bouch's Tay railway bridge – over which Queen Victoria had so graciously travelled, pausing on the far side to bestow a knighthood on the brilliant engineer – was overwhelmed by a violent storm, high winds causing the structure to collapse into the foaming river below. Unfortunately an engine and five coaches were on the bridge at the time and the 75 passengers and crew were drowned.

Today local people maintain that every year on the anniversary of the accident a ghost train crosses the bridge from the Edinburgh side. Its red rear lamp trails into the darkness and finally vanishes . . . just as the signalman saw the doomed train all those years ago.

The first Tay Bridge showed up the lack of expertise and foresight required for such a structure; no wind tunnels or sophisticated testing were available to the engineers in the late 1870s. Bouch's bridge was made mainly of wrought iron and did not allow for the movement so essential in bridges of that type.

The reappearance of the ill-fated train on the anniversary of the tragedy is not taken lightly by the local inhabitants, and there are many who will vouch for the authenticity of the phenomenon.

11
Lincolnshire signal box mysteries

The noise in the night

Elsham signal box is situated in a very remote part of the Lincolnshire countryside, and was the setting for strange experiences that baffled John Daubney when he had to take over the box as a relief signalman. One night shift in particular had mysterious overtones and still has not been explained.

Mr Daubney had been busy with a continuous stream of traffic, and when he was able to sit down for a brief breather, he received a telephone call from Control saying that some 20 young bullocks had got loose on the railway line heading in his direction and would he keep a look out for them, since trains and cattle do not mix! As it was very nearly dark, he did not relish the thought of trying to catch panic-stricken young bullocks on a railway line. In the event he saw no sign of the runaway animals, but later that night the local policeman called and took over the task of keeping a look-out.

Constable Hobbs left his bicycle leaning against the signal box wall and it screeched a little as it rubbed along the wall before coming to a rest; the sound was to remain in Mr Daubney's memory, for reasons that will be revealed. The constable stayed with John Daubney for the rest of his shift, and the signalman appreciated his company, but there was no sign of the errant beasts and, although both men peered regularly into the darkness and even went down to the lineside and checked, nothing was to be seen. Hopefully the cattle had been rounded up and were now safe.

The next night John Daubney resumed the night shift. No cattle to worry about tonight, he thought, and settled down to the job in hand. Everything was normal and the shift was going smoothly until about 3am, when (according to the medical profession) the human body is at its lowest ebb and we do not feel at our best. John heard a noise just like Constable Hobbs's bicycle screeching down the side of the box until it met an obstacle on the wall and stopped – or that is what it sounded like in the stillness of the night. 'Good,' thought the signalman, 'the policeman has called and it will be nice to have someone to say hello to.'

He went to the door, opened it and looked down the steps expecting to see Hobbs's burly figure emerge and climb the steps to meet him, but to John's surprise there was nobody there at all. He went round the corner of the building, shining his lamp, but nothing was to be seen.

'Strange', he thought, and attempted to puzzle out the cause of the noise. He decided that the occurrence could be resolved in daylight and that there was no point in groping about in the dark. However, once back upstairs in the box he could not leave the mystery alone and his mind conjured up all sorts of solutions, but analysing them brought no relief.

When he was relieved by the early turn man to take over the daylight duties, he mentioned the strange incident and asked him if he had any experiences to relate, but the other could think of nothing to either corroborate or add to the mystery. John later came back to the box and searched the land round the cabin to look for explanations, but nothing presented itself and the mystery remains to this day.

John Daubney is no fool and has sought the solution because he, like many others, looks for reasons for unexpected noises occurring at 3 o'clock in the morning.

Black Shuck's revenge

Places of human burial, be they cemeteries, church graveyards or Ancient Briton, Roman or Saxon burial barrows or mounds, are usually regarded as worthy of respect and reverence. To disturb the resting place of any person is regarded as defiling the dead, and this story concerns an archaeological exploration that quite accidentally set off a sinister sequence of events that was to cost a man his life and leave a whole community in turmoil.

Ted Smith owned a smallholding in a remote village in South Lincolnshire. He was able to live quite comfortably from the fruits of his labours, but he had always wanted just a little more land. Next to his holding was a small field of 1½ acres with a little mound in it. Ted felt that this field would be very useful and would enable him to extend his land just sufficient to give him, in his words, 'that bit extra'. The trouble was that the land belonged to a family who lived in London and owned parcels of land all over the country, and who had so far resisted all attempts to relinquish this innocuous piece of British soil.

Ted had therefore given up all hope of enlarging his holding and was concentrating his efforts on farming his existing soil, making a reasonable living from his multiplicity of vegetable crops, when a letter arrived one day explaining to him that if he still wanted to buy the adjoining land, the owners were interested in discussing the matter. Ted acted quickly and in time a deal was concluded and he became the owner of the 1½ acres of grassland.

After careful consideration Ted decided to deep-plough the land and prepare it for cultivation. One morning he drove a tractor and plough into the field and commenced the job. The land was hard and compacted but the plough shares carved through the earth cleanly and Ted knew that his labours would not be wasted. Suddenly Ted was aware that he was ploughing up something other than earth. He stopped, switched off the engine and climbed down. Turning round he saw a litter of bones strewn among the furrows. 'Good Lord,' he thought, 'I've hit a graveyard!'

On examining the bones he decided that they were very old, and the smell that exuded from them was particularly obnoxious. Ted decided to stop the operation and return home to discuss the find with his wife, Maureen, whose counsel was always common sense. Maureen was adamant. 'Leave them alone until someone who understands them has examined the site. Besides, they may be of some value or of interest to a museum, you never know.'

Ted agreed, but he decided to go and discuss the matter with his pal, Jim, who was the local signalman. Jim was very interested and begged Ted to allow him to have a look round. Their discussion was interrupted by the visit of Ted's Uncle Albert, who, at the age of 81, had wisdom to offer about most things. He was appraised on the situation and was asked his opinion.

'You have disturbed a burial site all right, but what is important is that you don't disturb it further,' he advised.

Jim was still curious. 'What about any valuables that may be buried with the remains? Could we get the archaeologists here for a dig?'

Uncle Albert shrugged his shoulders. 'It's up to Ted. It's his land, but if I were you both, I wouldn't disturb the dead – very dangerous!'

Ted laughed. 'Good Lord, what could the bones do to us? I'm not frightened – are you, Jim?'

Jim smiled. 'It could be very interesting. I like a mystery.'

Uncle Albert sighed. 'Well, I've warned you – don't meddle in things you don't understand.'

That night Ted and Jim met in the local pub to discuss the situation. Jim said, 'How about having another look at the site? We may uncover some valuables. It could be a Roman or Saxon burial ground and they were buried with their treasures. Perhaps we might uncover something of interest!'

Ted finished his drink. 'OK, we'll have another look, but don't tell anyone else or we'll have the whole village digging it up.'

Jim was free the following morning, and the two men stood looking at the bones. 'They smell a bit, Ted,' said Jim.

Ted felt an inexplicable shudder. 'Something unpleasant about the whole affair, don't you think?'

But Jim was excited. 'Come on,' he urged, 'let's see what else we can find.'

The two men started to dig down among the scattered bones to find other objects of interest. The work was hard and the sweat ran off their brows. They took great care and were concentrating on a small area, trying hard not to tread on the bones. After a lot of hard work they found that they were uncovering a complete skeleton. As it emerged, however, they found that they were looking not at a human, but an animal. Not a cow or horse, but the size of a sheep or goat. They rested and looked and sweated.

'What is it?' gasped Ted.

Jim thought. 'Well, it looks like a large dog – look at its head.'
The head was large and flattened, resembling that of a retriever.

'Tell you what,' said Jim, 'I'll take the skull and show it to Dave, the vet. He'll know what it could be.'

Ted agreed. 'Come on, let's go and have a cup of tea. Maureen was getting on to the museum about bringing an expert to have a look at the place.'

Maureen had some news. 'I've been in touch with the museum and someone is coming over next week. In the meantime they said don't touch anything.'

Ted explained that they had uncovered more bones, including the animal. He laughed, 'Jim's got the skull – he's going to show it to Dave, the vet.'

Maureen frowned. 'Do you think that's wise?'

Jim giggled. 'Course it's all right. It won't bite me. Anyway, I must be off. Thanks for the tea.'

Next morning Jim was on duty in the signal box. He had the skull in a plastic bag ready to consult Dave Smith, the local vet, when his shift ended. During a lull in the rail traffic, he opened the bag and had a good look at the object. It was hideous and awesome. It must have been a big animal; the jaws were large and powerful. Jim shuddered and put it back in the bag. Somehow he kept thinking about the whole affair and was no longer sure about the skull; should he have moved it?

When his shift ended, Jim made his way to Dave's surgery. The vet examined the skull and sucked his teeth.

'Must have been something big. I'd say it was a dog, but it's very, very old and that's as much as I can tell. I should put it back and cover it up. No point in disturbing the dead.'

Jim went home. He put the bag containing the skull in the shed with his bicycle. All the same, he found himself wondering about the strange animal and, almost as if he was under some strange influence, he could not get the events out of his mind. That night he was unable to sleep and it was only after taking some aspirins that he was able to get any rest. He was to commence night shifts and was not looking forward to it, with the strange thoughts and worries that were crowding his mind.

At lunchtime he went down to the pub, hoping to meet Ted.

After two pints he felt a bit better and Ted arrived. He did not say much but agreed that he had had queer thoughts and wondered whether they really were due to normal depression or the influence of the discovery. Both men felt better for the chat and company; they discussed Dave's opinion and Ted asked, 'By the way, where is the skull now?'

Jim told him and Ted said, 'I'll go and get it and put it back, then I'll cover it up until that museum chap comes.' Jim agreed.

Later that afternoon Jim arrived at Ted's house. 'Did you take the bag out of the shed, Ted?'

Ted looked surprised. 'No, I haven't had time,' he replied.

Jim gasped. 'Well it's gone. Who's got it now?' He looked at his watch. 'I shall have to go, Ted, I've got a lot to do before I go on shift. Perhaps it'll turn up – it's only a skull.'

Ted smiled. 'It can't do anyone any harm, so don't worry.'

That night Jim was a bit happier and did not think about the previous worries. He was busy and time was passing quickly. About 11pm he was aware that the wind was getting up and was buffeting the wooden signal box. The location of the box was remote, about 1½ miles from the village, but the line was busy and the box controlled a junction, so the signalman had to have his wits about him.

Later the wind dropped and everything seemed peaceful. Jim was reading the daily newspaper and enjoying a cup of tea when he became aware of a noise outside the box. He thought, 'Hello, is someone coming up to keep me company?'; he went to the door and looked out down the steps. The night was cool and he shivered. He was about to turn and go inside when he became aware of a large shape below. He gasped. It was a big black dog with large orb-like eyes gazing up at him with a malevolent gaze. Then it bayed and Jim was stricken with terror. He leapt back into the cabin and locked the door.

He sank into his chair and tried to compose himself. He fancied that he could hear the thing moving about outside and he was glad that the door was locked. Whose dog was it? He had never seen it before. Luckily there was no more traffic on the line for the time being. He smoked incessantly until dawn lit the sky, then he cautiously looked around, feeling a little better.

Eventually his relief came up the steps. 'Everything OK, Jim?'

'Everything's fine,' Jim replied, and went home.

When he had had his breakfast, he went to the shed, opened the door and was nearly knocked out by the overpowering smell. He began to tidy the shed and look around for the plastic bag, but there was no sign and he could not puzzle out where it could have gone. Then he had a thought.

'Uncle Albert often comes to borrow various garden tools – perhaps he's got it. Yes, that's it. I'll go and ask him later.'

After dinner the sun shone and Jim cycled down to Uncle Albert's cottage, situated near the railway line, but the old man was not in. Jim looked in the windows to see if he was around, but nobody was there.

That night the weather worsened, the wind blew up a gale, and it poured with rain. Jim heard noises on the steps, but when he investigated there was nothing there. Then his next train was belled and he accepted it into his section, setting the signals. As the heavy diesel locomotive with its oil tank train slowly passed the box, he suddenly heard a noise outside again. He looked out and there it was, the animal, with its great yellow eyes and the epitome of evil in its gaze. He slammed the cabin door, only to hear the hurried application of train brakes. He could see that the tail light of the oil train had stopped. Something had happened!

He threw the signals to danger, sent the emergency bell code and tore down the steps, his lamp and red flag in his hand. The guard of the oil train was running towards him. Jim shone his torch – the man's face was ashen.

'An old man,' gasped the guard. 'He threw himself under us, he must have done.'

Jim ran to the scene. There under a wagon was the body of Uncle Albert, and clutched in his hand was a plastic bag containing the splintered remains of an animal's skull. . .

Other signal box mysteries

By virtue of their often remote locations, signal boxes are the sort of places that are likely to be the settings of experiences of a supernatural nature, so it is no surprise that most signalmen have tales of mystery to tell. They are not often told in the first person, usually the third person, but they are authentic all the same.

After all, who are we to disbelieve events that have occurred in a lonely box during a night shift when the wind is wailing and buffeting the timber structure? The noises that sometimes pervade the silence beggar description, while the signalmen are, remember, level-headed, intelligent people who are hand-picked to do a responsible, onerous job.

One box in Lincolnshire was home to a poltergeist or mischievous ghost, but it was of a gentle nature and although it moved cups of tea and generally showed its playfulness, it never hurt anyone and was not vicious or dangerous. No one knew much about it except that it was always there and was therefore accepted. Pencils would hover in mid-air and windows would open and shut; the door would open, and the lights would go on and off.

The signal box at Kirton Lindsey was the subject of an unexplained occurrence that was to baffle everyone. Footsteps were heard coming up the steps, but no one ever appeared at the door. In the end it became an accepted phenomenon, the only explanation offered being that the blasting in the nearby limestone quarry was to blame for the movement, which suggested settlement. It was a convenient theory, but was it really the cause?

What, we may ask, caused the gate locking lever in Holton-le-Moor signal box to ease itself out of the frame slowly but determinedly, without rational cause or explanation, even after thorough examination?

Again, how is it that Claxby box, locked up and deserted, could give the 5-5-5 bell code ('Opening of signal box') to Market Rasen?

These events are just a few of the unexplained happenings in Lincolnshire signal boxes. Who are we to disbelieve them?

12
The little old guard

A strange apparition was witnessed by a lady a few years ago on a section of track between Barking and Upminster in Essex. Journeys at that time were subject to many delays owing to permanent way maintenance work, and the passengers were heartily fed up. Several times they had had to step down from the train and walk along the track to the nearest station; they were all anxious to get home and any delay was unwelcome.

On this particular occasion the lady who kindly offered me this account was returning home from a hospital visit. It was around 6pm, and very dark, when suddenly the train began to slow down to a crawl. 'What now?' thought the passengers. Then to everyone's surprise they saw on the side of the track a little old man, perhaps in his 70s, wearing an old-fashioned waistcoat and jacket, standing in a brick arch-shaped wall recess and looking anxiously at the train. As it drew near he took a step forward, shining his lantern with its green light above his head as if to give the driver the 'All Clear'. Our correspondent smiled to herself, no doubt thinking that the railway must be short of staff if they had to bring such an old man out of his back garden to work the system.

Since that occasion she has looked many times to find the recess in which the old man was standing, but without success. It simply is not there – even the wall does not exist. The whole scene was as clear as a bell to her, but on reflection it would seem as if it was part of an earlier railway system. She is sure that she was privileged to witness a scene from the past in startling clarity, and it is an experience that has continued to baffle her ever since.

13
Tulse Hill station

*M*r Jack Hallam's excellent book *Ghosts of London* tells of the unexplained sounds of heavy footsteps heard by staff at night at Tulse Hill station in South London. Footsteps are heard ascending the stairs to platform 1, passing clean through the locked barrier gates and proceeding along the platform.

The footsteps are said to be those of an unfortunate platelayer who was killed shortly after the introduction of the electric trains. That fateful night he ascended the stairs, passed through the barrier, greeted the porter on duty and walked down on to the track. It was a cold and blustery night, and knowing that a down steam-hauled train was due, he stepped on to the up line instead of the safety of the trackside. It is thought that the sound of the approaching steam train and the wind prevented him from being aware of the electric train's presence, and he was run down and killed.

However, it seems that he was so attached to his job that he still wants to keep an eye on his old workplace. The past tragedy thus lingers on, and certain people will not go on the station after dark.

14
The broken-hearted lover

*M*r Cubbage was an Indian, dark and very handsome. He had settled in Ireland and through his shrewd business ability and financial acumen had become very wealthy. Just after the Second World War he bought a large mansion, restored it to its former magnificent glory and settled down to enjoy his wealth. There was only one thing he lacked and that was a wife. Mr Cubbage must have seemed a good catch with his fine house, handsome looks and his obvious wealth. Could any girl resist these assets?

Mr Cubbage, however, was very circumspect in his choice of lady friends, and realised that he could easily be the target for any 'gold-digging' female. He looked around very carefully and finally met a young lady, whom we will call Coleen, with whom he fell headlong in love. Their mutual affection was genuine and Mr Cubbage was overjoyed at his good fortune. He entertained his young lady to the best things in life, heaping upon her presents of jewellery, furs, motor cars, travel, expensive restaurants, days out hunting – in other words he was trying to sweep the young lady clean off her pretty feet.

Mr Cubbage wanted to get married at once. He wanted an answer quickly; he was not used to delay of any kind and kept up the pressure, forcibly yet kindly. He loved Coleen with every breath in his body, and would do anything to persuade her to be his wife.

Coleen, however, although she loved Mr Cubbage, wanted time to think things over and would gently scold him for his haste. She listened to his amorous overtures of love, never doubting his sincerity, but she still wanted to be sure before she said 'yes', and she tried gently to tell him so. After a lot of thought she decided to go to stay with friends in England to think things over.

Mr Cubbage was most distraught at Coleen's decision, and bombarded her with letters and flowers; he could not wait for her return and for her to say the one word that would make her his wife. But Coleen was enjoying herself in England. She thought of Mr Cubbage a lot, but was still reluctant to commit herself just yet.

Mr Cubbage was by this time almost demented – he had to know Coleen's decision, so he wrote an impassioned letter begging her to accept his proposal of marriage. Furthermore, he added what might be construed as an ultimatum, but couched in the gentlest possible terms: if he had not had a reply from her before noon on the last day of the week (which meant by return of post), he would trouble her no more.

On that fateful day the first delivery of post came and went with no letter. Mr Cubbage, his heart heavy with disappointment and sadness, left his mansion, walked the short distance to the main Portadown to Lurgan railway line and awaited the passing of the next train. He walked up and down the track impatiently. He had made up his mind. He was going to lie down in front of the train. His life was meaningless without Coleen; she had not replied to his entreaties, so he would end it all.

Mr Cubbage heard the engine whistle. The train was slowing for a signal, then he heard it pick up speed again. Now a broken, weeping figure, he lay down on the rail and waited for the train to end his life and his earthly troubles. The driver of the train did not see him until it was too late; the engine literally cut him in half, and he must have died instantly.

The tragic irony of the story is that the sailings between England and Ireland on that particular day had been delayed owing to bad weather, so the mail was held up. It so happened that the very train that ended Mr Cubbage's life was carrying that delayed mail, and in one of the mail bags was a letter from Coleen agreeing to Mr Cubbage's proposal of marriage and saying that she was coming home to her lover.

To this day the ghost of Mr Cubbage walks the coaches of many trains on the line, searching for his beloved Coleen; he has been seen often by many people in the district. He also walks the railway tracks near the spot at which he was killed, a sobbing, totally heart-broken figure. He is said to sink to his knees on the track and wait for the train to end his life; train crews used to look out for the shadowy figure and shudder.

15
The suicidal student

About the turn of the century, Ian Watson, a young medical student at Aberdeen University, ran into financial difficulties. His father, a well-to-do fish merchant in Fraserburgh, had no idea of a student's expenses at a university like Aberdeen. Ian was a clever young man who had worked very hard to achieve his place at the higher seat of learning, but he found it very difficult to manage on the pittance that his father allowed him. His father's idea of universities was extremely limited, possibly as a result of his own education, which had been one of strict discipline and the basic 'three Rs'; he had left school at 13 and had had to work hard for very little reward. To give him credit, though, he had fought his way to the top and had made good.

Ian Watson was a dedicated, somewhat highly strung young man whose intelligence would have enabled him to have passed his final exams had his father realised the necessity of a reasonable allowance. His father obviously did not appreciate his son's undoubted abilities, for Ian's request for more money met with scorn. 'Come home and work with me, lad – don't mess about with those books, I need you here,' his father said.

Ian was very upset by his father's intransigent attitude, but he knew what he wanted to do, which was to pursue his studies by every means possible, although by now doubts were beginning to cloud his mind. Inevitably a feeling of despair enveloped him and he began to feel quite helpless; his heart was in his studies and he knew that if he could manage financially he could achieve his academic rewards, but the insufficient amounts of money his father allowed him did not permit any freedom to relax after his studies had ended. He could see no way out and in his anguish he began to think of taking his own life.

The method he would use would have to be quick and simple. After some consideration he decided that he would lie on the railway line and let a train end his life. He then remembered a high bridge over the railway at Kirkston of Philorth, and decided to throw himself off the parapet instead of lying down on the track. He would time it just right and throw himself in front of the branch-line train; he knew it did not go very fast, but it would do. . .

In the early evening of the next day he dressed himself in his best suit with a clean shirt and stiff collar. He looked at himself in the mirror – yes, he looked good, almost handsome. One must die with dignity.

He had quite a long way to walk to the bridge, but there was plenty of time; he had taken the trouble to find out the train times and he had worked out when the train would arrive at the bridge – about 9pm. When he arrived at the bridge he walked over it and back again, then looked over the parapet at the shining metals curving away around the bend. Everything was quiet, the moon had come out and there was just a touch of frost in the air.

Ian climbed up on to the parapet and sat swinging his legs and humming a tune; he felt quite happy now, almost cheerful, and he began to wonder why he was thinking of suicide. He had everything to live for really – he could manage on the money his mean father allowed him. Should he go through with his intention to end his life?

'That's what I'm here for,' an inner voice shouted. 'Don't be silly, why do something stupid like hurling yourself in front of a train?' The thoughts crowded into his mind. He looked at his pocket watch – it showed 8.55pm, not long to go now. He was in a turmoil of doubt – what should he do?

He lit a cigarette and watched the smoke wreathe into the night air. He enjoyed his smoke, then climbed on to the parapet and started to walk along its broad surface. He would walk over and back, then go home – life was still sweet in spite of father's

mean ways. He could hear the muffled sound of the train as it
plodded round the bend. Happier now, Ian ran and danced on
the parapet: 'Come on train, I'm not afraid of you.'

'The train rumbled nearer, and Ian was still jigging about on
the parapet. He could see the smokebox lamp flickering, then as
the train reached the bridge the smoke enveloped him as he
danced his Highland jig. He lost his balance and fell on to the
locomotive; the force of the fall did its lethal work, and Ian
Watson was dead.

The train braked hard at the fireman's shout of 'There's a man
on the line!', and the few passengers on the train were thrown
from their seats. The loco crew ran up to the inert body, but it
was too late – the man was dead, his head at a strange angle.
They carried the body to the brake compartment and carried on
their journey; others had jumped from that bridge and there
would be more.

The unfortunate tragedy was a talking point in the district for
several weeks, but slowly became forgotten. Then a reminder of
the tragedy occurred during the First World War when a Polish
soldier, walking over the bridge one starlit night, saw the wraith
of a man dancing on the parapet. Then smoke obscured the
bridge, and a sound of escaping steam and a cry took the man
from the observer's sight. The soldier looked over the parapet
and saw to his horror the vague heap of a body. He scrambled
down the bank, but as he approached the vision slowly faded –
there was no one there. This experience had such a dramatic
effect on the Pole that he hanged himself some days later.

No further reports have been documented, but possibly people
who have seen a replay of the awful scene wish to remain silent
rather than discuss the macabre subject. In the 1920s a local man
was in a terrible state of nerves and he too visited the bridge with
the one thought in his mind. Yes, he did commit suicide on that
bridge, but he drank from a bottle of lysol, a poisonous
disinfectant, which would have meant a swift but painful end. I
wonder if he is also seen on that fateful bridge?

16
Footsteps in the ballast

*T*his recent story, quite unexplained, was related to me by Mr G. Leslie, who is employed by British Rail in the London area. It concerns the sound of footsteps in the ballast; no one is seen but the sounds are quite distinct, and one respects Mr Leslie's account, being someone who certainly does not believe in the supernatural, preferring to find a logical explanation for this sort of occurrence.

Mr Leslie had been to a railway staff party in The Flint pub, which is situated across the road from High Wycombe station. He admits to having had a drink but he says he was by no means 'under the influence'. At about 11.20pm he left the party to catch his train back to his home at Beaconsfield. As a northbound train had just left, the station was deserted. Mr Leslie's train was to leave from platform 3 on the far side of the station, which is approached by a long subway. On arriving at the platform somewhat early for his train, he found himself completely alone, although this did not disturb him.

The night was still but a mist was descending slowly. He was standing looking towards the down platforms when he suddenly heard footsteps on the ballast approaching him. Mr Leslie was completely sober and is not given to flights of imagination, so he screwed up his eyes to look for the source of the footsteps; he could not see the feet but heard them quite distinctly passing him in the ballast below. At this point some other people arrived to catch the train and his attention turned to them for a split second; within that time the sound of the crunching footsteps disappeared into the night.

Some time later, after Christmas, Mr Leslie was on High Wycombe station again and was talking to one of the station staff. He told him of his experience and was interested to learn that the phenomenon was by no means unknown; his colleague went on to relate another incident involving footsteps that he heard outside the office, but when he opened the door to investigate no one was there. On another occasion he gave chase to someone running down the platform, but when he reached the platform end whoever it was had vanished. Mr Leslie was now certain that he was dealing with a facet of the supernatural!

17
The mystery lights

*P*aranormal experiences never happen to some people, which is why they cannot understand other people who are able to experience supernatural events. Research has only scratched the surface of paranormal and supernatural phenomena, so we are left with odd cases of events that occur when least expected.

Such an occurrence happened to Mr R. J. Woodward of Hinckley, who with his wife and daughter was travelling home around midnight along the A5, the Roman Watling Street. They had been visiting friends and had enjoyed their evening; the time had passed quickly so it was rather late when they set off for home.

They were proceeding north on the A5 near Lutterworth when Mr Woodward's attention was suddenly drawn to what he first thought were three buses standing nose-to-tail. Before he could say anything Mrs Woodward exclaimed, 'Isn't it strange to see a train at this time of night?'

Mr Woodward knew the area well and there were no existing railways here at all; only traces of the trackbed of the old Rugby-Leicester line. Being something of a railway enthusiast, he thought that the lights were spread out as they might be in old non-corridor stock, with three windows to each compartment, but there was just the lights, no outline of a locomotive or the carriages.

The line had closed some 30 years before, but there was never a track just where the lights were positioned. Distance is deceptive, especially at night; might there have been a branch line? The phenomenon lasted perhaps 30 to 45 seconds, long enough for a firm but puzzling impression to be gained.

18
The haunted recording studio

The Horizon Recording Studio used to be housed in what was an old Victorian railway building in Warwick Road, Coventry. A series of strange events has happened in the building, which can be traced to the ghost of an old railwayman, and, about 20 years later, the spirit of an art student who unfortunately died from drink and drugs after he attended the celebration party to launch the studio.

Mr Paul Craddock, a director of Horizon, kindly sent me some details of the paranormal events that have earned the studio a certain reputation for unexpected phenomena. Certainly some famous recording artists have had frightening moments when they have been nudged and brushed past by these two ghosts. Mr Craddock thinks that the older man is dominating the art student.

The young student was about 19 when he died; he had worked hard on the dramatic murals in the studio before he fatally tried mixing drugs with drink. The building itself was formerly railway offices, and the old railwayman probably worked there; certainly his presence is very evident.

As with most supernatural occurrences, one never knows just when something is going to happen, and this is the case in the studio. Strange sounds are heard over the loudspeaker monitors, and a recording session can be spoiled completely by these two ghosts: lights go on and off, doors open and shut on their own, the shadow of a man's head is sometimes seen. During recording sessions many unnerving things can happen, such as the sound of heavy breathing down musicians' necks, and a feeling of being brushed past. Footsteps are heard all over the building, causing apprehension and expectancy in those visitors who have heard about the phenomena but haven't experienced them.

A famous recording artist with the group Fleetwood Mac was really frightened by one of the ghostly duo and he swears that he will never come into the building again, such was his experience.

19
Last across

*T*his story concerns two young boys who experienced the recurrence of a terrible death involving a young and irresponsible lad who used to play 'chicken' with a motorcycle on an ungated railway crossing. This lethal game is often called 'last across', the idea being to see how close you can be to a train before it hits you or you can get out of the way. Of course, at last a train caught the boy and killed him in a horrible way.

One very hot night in June 1982 Dave and Tony went fishing in a remote area of wasteland that bordered a disused railway line. A large pond was the boys' delight and they would travel the considerable distance to the 'newty pond', as it was nicknamed, to sit and wait for the fish to bite. To reach the pond they had to walk though two dark, gloomy plantations, which after dark were very spooky, and the boys were always pleased to get through them.

However, boys will be boys, and they enjoyed the fresh air and the sport of fishing; in fact, they had been known to fish after dark at the newty pond, which was very illegal! But the fishing trip that hot and humid night was to be something different, and it would frighten and distress the boys.

They found their usual post at the pond near the gated level crossing on the old trackbed and set up their gear. However, there was nothing stirring at the pond that night, so at around 10pm, after wandering around looking for frogs and newts, they decided to call it a day. They gathered together their rods and landing nets and set off for home.

Suddenly they heard the hum of a motorcycle coming towards them, and they both saw the machine being ridden towards the level crossing. It was travelling at high speed and the boys thought that it was going to hit them; the rider was crouched over the handlebars, obviously unaware of the boys. They threw down their fishing gear and ran as the motorcycle leapt over the embankment and crashed into the deep ditch some 15 feet beyond. The boys heard the crash and ran as fast as they could to get help from the police and ambulance, but when the authorities arrived they only found the boys' fishing tackle where they had dumped it in such haste.

The boys never went to the pond again, but did hear reports from other anglers that screams and shouts came from the ditch on the other side of the old trackbed, together with the eerie sound of a noisy motorcycle being ridden flat out towards the railway line.

About a year later one of the boys met an old lady who lived not far from the pond, and they were discussing the strange happenings when the lady said, 'I can tell you a bit about it.' She then proceeded to tell them about the crazy motorcyclist.

'He was mad on motorbikes and would tear around on that wasteland near the railway, bent on killing himself, I'd say. He'd play last across with the trains. No wonder he was killed by a train – he had many near misses. He always appears on the anniversary of his death and you'll see the whole incident in startling detail.'

I understand that the deep ditch into which the boy and his motorcycle crashed on that fateful night is referred to as 'deadman's ditch', a horrific reminder of a foolhardy game that cost a young man his life. One of the boys, now an adult, tells me that even today he shivers at the memory that is etched on his brain of being chased by a ghost on a motorcycle. . .

20
Dicky o'Tunstead

The legend relating to Dicky o'Tunstead caused the London & North Western Railway Company many problems and succeeded in forcing that concern to reconsider their plans for their new line between Chapel-en-le-Frith and Buxton.

Dicky o' Tunstead is a celebrated skull that resided at Tunstead Farm in Derbyshire for some three and a half centuries. He found fame in poetry and prose, and also had the reputation of being a supernatural Robin Hood; documentary evidence of the exploits attributed to him is legion. All attempts to evict Dicky from his rightful home have met with considerable misfortune, and disturbance of such a nature that he has quickly been restored to the farm.

Tunstead Farm overlooks Coomb Reservoir between Chapel-en-le-Frith and Whaley Bridge. The LNWR's engineers had planned to take their new line across land belonging to the farm, despite objections from the owners, and this is where Dicky became involved.

It was originally intended to make an embankment across the Coomb Valley, which was to be pierced by a bridge to accommodate a roadway. However, soon after work began it was found that there were serious problems in making a secure, stable base for the embankment, and progress was thus brought to a halt.

Eventually, however, the navvies and engineers overcame the difficulties and the bridge was erected over the road and the foundations of the embankment laid. Then before work was finally complete the arch of the bridge collapsed and the embankment on either side was thrown up, wrecking the whole project. A great deal of time and money had been spent rebuilding the works necessary to complete the job, but such were the difficulties experienced that the whole project became completely impracticable and the LNWR conceded defeat and altered the route of the line to exclude the land at Tunstead Farm.

The new work also involved the construction of a road over a quarter of a mile long, but no unexpected difficulties were experienced, either with this or the realigned route of the railway.

Of course the sceptics and doubters will sneer at the influence exercised by Dicky on the affair, saying that the former route was unsuitable and geographically unstable, and they will point out that such conditions have been overcome in other parts, for example the West Highland, Liverpool & Manchester and Settle & Carlisle lines, but then those conversant with Dicky o'Tunstead will continue to believe that it is his malign influence, which kept the rails away from Tunstead Farm.

21
The Luck of Edenhall

*T*here is an interesting legend behind the London & North Western Railway's 'Whitworth' Class locomotive No 90, unusually named *The Luck of Edenhall*. The name was derived from Eden Hall, a house that stands near Penrith on the former LNWR West Coast Main Line, and also within sight of the Midland Railway's rival Settle & Carlisle line. Eden Hall was the family seat of the Cumbrian family of Musgrave from the days of King Henry VI, and the 'Luck' is an heirloom, a beautifully enamelled and engraved glass goblet with Moorish-style decorative work on its surfaces.

How it came into the Musgrave family is a strange tale. One day, when the family butler went to draw water from St Cuthbert's well in the grounds of Eden Hall, he came across a company of fairies dancing, and in their midst was a cup of painted glass. The butler seized the glass, whereupon the fairies tried to regain it, but realising that they were no match for this mortal they finally abandoned the struggle and vanished, leaving the butler with the glass cup and, according to a ballad by the German poet Uhland, this warning:

> 'If that glass either break or fall
> Farewell to the Luck of Eden Hall.'

Ever since that time the fate of the Musgrave family and the strangely beautiful glass goblet have been regarded as inextricably entwined. The vessel is described as being about 6 inches tall, and it has been suggested that it may have been used as a chalice, and might have originated in Spain or Syria and been brought home to England from one of the Crusades. But whatever the origins, the warning of the fairy folk has never been left to chance and the 'Luck' still exists; it is either locked away in a strong room on the premises or, according to some accounts, stored safely in the custody of the Bank of England.

Eden Hall was extensively rebuilt in 1935 or thereabouts, and much of the original fabric removed; today it is a girls' school.

The poet Longfellow's version of the Uhland ballad runs thus:

> 'This Glass of Flashing Crystal Tall
> Gave to my Sires, The Fountain Sprite
> She wrote in it, "If this Glass Doth Fall
> Farewell Then Luck of Eden Hall"'

It is from the last line of this work that the LNWR derived the name for their locomotive.

22
The spectral train of Kyle

Some supernatural manifestations are regarded as portents of good or evil, and one such occurrence was the 'spectral train of Kyle'. In the 17th century a famous visionary and seer, locally know as the Brahan Seer, predicted 'That the day will come when every stream will have its bridge, balls of fire will pass rapidly up and down the Strath of Peffery, carriages without horses will cross the country from sea to sea.' This prophecy came true when in 1870 the Dingwall & Skye Railway opened its line from Dingwall on the eastern coast of Scotland to Strome Ferry on the west, on the shores of the waters of Loch Carron. A further 27 years were to elapse before the railway reached its ultimate terminus at the Kyle of Lochalsh.

However, the arrival of the railway was foreshadowed by the appearance of a spectral train whose large black locomotive was seen rushing along the lonely Highland road with headlights blazing before suddenly veering off into the hills. It would seem that this apparition became a regular occurrence, to such an extent that the coachman who operated a public conveyance until the opening of the railway to Kyle of Lochalsh would only operate in daylight.

23
French Drove & Gedney Hill

This quaintly named station, originally just French Drove, was opened by the Great Northern Railway on 2 September 1867, and in 1882 became part of the GN&GE Joint line. Situated south of Postland (Crowland) on the Spalding to March line near the point where the GNR line crossed the M&GN Joint line at Murrow, refuge sidings were provided to handle the considerable volume of freight traffic, mainly generated by local farmers with their produce. Passenger traffic was profitable until BR decided that this facility should be withdrawn as from 11 September 1961, but the goods traffic continued until the ultimate closure of the station on 5 October 1964, a victim of the Beeching Axe.

After closure the station was offered for sale as a dwelling house. The line was still open but run down and neglected, with fewer and fewer trains travelling over the weed-covered, rusting tracks. After a while, general deterioration having started, a buyer was found, and Mr Harold Caunt and his son moved in to restore the structure and make it into a home.

However, the Caunts were to experience several unwanted, bewildering and totally unexpected events, but let Mr Caunt explain.

'One fine day, being in need of provisions, my eldest son Terry and I cycled to the village shop in Gedney Hill. While being served by the young lady behind the counter, who had noticed that we were strangers, we were asked from whence we came.

"French Drove station," we replied.

On hearing our reply she went deathly white. "Oh dear," she said eventually, "you don't want to live there, the place is haunted."

Now, being of a practical disposition and having lived in many strange places, I wasn't going to be put off by local village rumours about ghosts. We carried on the restoration work at the station; there was much to do and we were kept very busy and involved with our work.

Subsequent events, however, were to remind us of the shop girl's warning. The mail in those days was delivered by a post lady on a bike, usually at around 8.30am. One day we were having breakfast when we heard a woman's voice from near the foot of the stairs in the hall. Expecting to find the post lady at the door, Terry went to collect the mail only to find no one in view. He looked around but there was no sign of anyone. Puzzled, he returned to report that there was no one there.

It so happened that the post was late that day. We thought about the event carefully, as we certainly did not consider ourselves as fools, nor did we imagine things of this nature. We had definitely heard a woman's voice, that was certain, so we had to accept the fact that something funny was going on and we would have to see what happened in the future.

Some time later we had a visit from a young man who worked for BR and was on holiday revisiting some of the stations that he had worked at in the past. During a conversation in which I mentioned the mystery of the woman's voice, he explained that many years ago a station master at French Drove had committed suicide by hanging himself from a hook in the ceiling of the room above the ticket office. His poor distressed wife died shortly afterwards and it transpired that she used to help her husband in his duties. It became her job to close the station at night, and in the dark winter nights she used to carry a stable lantern to enable her to find her way around the dark corners of the station.

Our visitor told us that her ghost had been seen by several local people at certain times of the year. So, when a lighted lamp wobbled along the track one dark, winter's night, we really cringed in terror. Luckily there was an explanation for this occurrence – we found that the husband of the crossing-keeper further up the line, who worked at Perkins Engines, rode his bike along the track when on his night shift, and brought it up on to the platform to leave it under the signal box to await a lift to work; hence the wobbly light.

However, the mystery of the woman's voice remained a worrying event that often caused a shiver to run down our spines. Also, the stories of the sighting of the ghost of the station master's wife were confirmed by the local residents, many of whom wouldn't come near the station after dark. So what now? Let us hope that the restless ghost of a distraught wife has found peace at last; certainly no logical reason has been offered to explain the strange events at French Drove & Gedney Hill station, and it will continue to baffle and tantalise our enquiring minds for some time to come.'

24
Heard but not seen

The unmistakable sound of a train 'working hard against the grade' three months after a line's closure is what my correspondent Mr Bernard Essex heard early one morning. As Mr Essex observes, to make up a convincing faked ghost story is difficult, but to tell the incredible truth is easy because what Mr Essex tells me is, he is sure, absolutely true.

Mr Essex lives in the Warwickshire village of Studley and about a mile east of the former trackbed of the railway that ran from Redditch in a generally southerly direction towards Alcester, Evesham and Ashchurch. All rail services south of Redditch were terminated in June 1964 and until that time Mr Essex could hear quite clearly from his house the sounds of trains, most of which were steam-hauled when services ceased, after which time naturally the familiar sounds were no more, just a memory. But were they?

About three months after the final day of operation, Mr Essex was getting up at about 6am one morning. He was wide awake and dressing, and all was still and quiet, when suddenly on the early morning breeze came the faint sound of a steam locomotive on the now closed railway line, working hard with a short cut-off as it fought the familiar gradient. Mr Essex was utterly amazed and quickly opened the window to investigate.

The sound became louder until the final familiar crescendo, then it died away gradually to a faint whisper until it had gone, just as if it had been proceeding normally on its journey. Mr Essex assures me that the exhaust beats were clearly audible, and the sounds of steam issuing from the cylinder drain cocks and the clank of the valve gear were clearly heard. The experience lasted for about 3 minutes.

Later that day Mr Essex phoned Redditch station to ask the staff about the possibility of trains running on the old line north towards Birmingham, and Mr Essex told them what he had heard. Eventually he spoke to the station master who was very interested yet amused by the story. He explained that although the track south of Redditch was still in situ, all the points and controls for single-line working and the exit at the south end had been taken out, and it would have been impossible for a train to leave or enter Redditch at that end.

Mr Essex of course searched for a logical explanation of this mystery; the only other operating part of British Railways in the area was and still is the former Great Western line at Henley-in-Arden, about 8 miles to the east of Mr Essex's home. He assures me that it is completely inaudible, so we can discard that theory.

Even a practical joker playing a recording of a steam train operating over that line would have had to be very clever to produce a convincing effect, especially from a static position.

Mr Essex was, he believes, the only person who heard the unexplained sounds, and he says that although his experience cannot be corroborated he believes that there would be no point in making up such a story. So we are left with the mysterious sounds that would seem to defy any rational explanation.

25
Second sight?

*I*am indebted to Mr M. Houghton of Bolton for a very strange mystery from his boyhood, for which to this day there would appear to be no explanation. One can only think that he somehow became involved in a kind of time warp that was to continue to bewilder him some 30 years later.

It happened when he was 13, and very keen on train-spotting; he would, like most boys of his age, go anywhere to get engine numbers. He was an expert on the different types of engines, where they came from, where they were going – in fact a young authority on anything to do with trains. This incident took place in 1950. It was a Sunday evening in August and the location was Northenden Junction on the former Cheshire Lines where the main line into Stockport (Tiviot Dale) and the LNWR branch into Stockport (Edgeley) diverged.

'On this particular Sunday, as on most Sundays, the signal box at Northenden Junction was switched out and the signals left clear for the main line to and from Tiviot Dale. The next box to the west (Baguley) was also apparently switched out – it invariably was on a Sunday – and the distant signal was showing clear for the whole of the time that I was at the location. This left a very long section of line between Skelton Junction to the west, which in my recollection was always open, and I think Heaton Mersey to the east, towards Tiviot Dale.

As I was aware that excursions to and from the Lancashire coast very often passed through Northenden on a Sunday, I cycled along there to see whether there would be any action. I positioned myself on a road bridge adjacent to Northenden Junction signal box. It was a very clear summer evening, visibility was excellent and there was full light. I waited on the bridge for about an hour, and although I was very patient I then began to fidget. I wanted to see some action – besides, I had to be home soon as I had a paper round to do early the following morning. No one was about; I looked up and down the line, but there was nothing in sight.

I was just about to pack up and go home when I suddenly saw the smoke of a train approaching from the direction of Skelton Junction. I positioned myself on the bridge parapet, safely of course, to get a good look at the engine and the length of the train. When it came into view, the engine was a Stanier Class '5', or 'Black Five' as the train-spotters called them. It was hauling a train of five coaches, and when it reached my position I noted the engine's number on the smokebox door as 44813. It was travelling at a leisurely pace, probably between 40 and 45mph. I paid no more attention to it as it passed under the bridge, but recorded the number in the pocket book that I always carried with me on these trips.

I then looked up and down the line to see if anything else was in sight and noticed to my surprise another plume of smoke coming from the same direction as the other train. I quickly looked to see if I could see the last train but of course it had disappeared. I couldn't believe that two trains could follow each other so close in so long a section, but it was another train all right and I was interested to see if it was another passenger working.

Although at my tender age I did not understand the complexities of signalling, something told me that all was not as it should be, but by now the train was getting nearer and I was bent on taking the number of the loco.

I remained in my position on the bridge, and as the train approached I saw that it was again a 'Black Five' hauling five carriages, same as the last one. Now for the number – I peered at the smokebox number plate, and to my surprise it read 44813. I was puzzled. The train was again running at a leisurely 40-45mph, same as the last one. I thought, very strange! I opened my pocket book, and there on the page was the number of the previous loco, 44813.

I couldn't believe it. It would appear that I had been caught up in something queer at that time, although the thought of a time warp did not enter my mind. Years later I did wonder about the possibility of a time warp, but even then was not sure what one of these things was.

The possibility of a mistake on my part never entered my mind; at 13 train-spotting was a very serious business and we were all eagle-eyed, and mistakes did not happen.

Over the years I thought from time to time about those mysterious happenings, and the memory is still very clear in my mind. Although I have been over and over it in my mind the circumstances remain completely unsolved. One thing is certain – what were two trains doing running so close together? That alone is a complete mystery.'

26
The train in the night

The village of West Dereham lies near a branch line that used to serve four stations, Denver, Ryston, Abbey & West Dereham and the terminus at Stoke Ferry; the branch left the former Great Northern line running south from King's Lynn to Ely at Denver, almost halfway between the two larger places. Passenger traffic was withdrawn on 22 September 1930 and final closure to goods and the cessation of railway services took place on 31 January 1966.

The location of our story was originally known as Abbey, then Abbey for West Dereham from 1 January 1886. The name was changed again on 1 July 1923 to Abbey & West Dereham and that is how it stayed until closure of the station.

Mr A. Dixon of West Bridgford near Nottingham writes to tell me of a very strange occurrence that happened to him and his wife while they were living in West Dereham in 1954-5. Mr Dixon worked at a local farm on the outskirts of the village; in those days the station only had the benefit of a goods service, which I suspect only ran when demand warranted it. The farmers used it to convey their produce, and general goods were carried on occasions.

One night Mr Dixon woke with a start – he could hear a noise. He leapt out of bed and peered out of the window. The Dixons' house commanded a view over the railway where it ran through the village. Mrs Dixon, also waking, wanted to know what the excitement was about, and soon joined her husband at the window. They could both hear a train coming towards the village, the clear night amplifying the unmistakable sound of an approaching steam engine. They looked at each other, peered out of the window again, then they saw it – an engine pulling two coaches passing slowly along the rusting line.

As it slowly passed out of sight the Dixons looked at each other in puzzlement – where would a passenger train be running to at around 3am, who would be opening the gates and operating the signals? Still wondering, they returned to bed.

The following day Mr Dixon mentioned the incident to his workmates on the farm. They looked at each other and grinned. One man said, 'You've been dreaming – no passenger train has run down this line for years.'

But the Dixons were adamant; they knew what they had seen, it had been very real to them, and neither could be accused of romancing or being under the influence of drink. They went to have a look at the line; it was very rusty and overgrown and there was no sign of anything having travelled on it recently, not since the last goods train.

No explanation has been offered to solve this incident, so it is likely to remain an unanswered mystery.

27
A stranger in the fog

*T*his story is timeless and loses nothing in the repeating. Although it dates from 1917, its drama is retained and it could have happened many years later.

Henry Kirkup did not believe in ghosts. He was a contented man, fond of his pint of beer and a bet on the horses, but one thing was absolutely certain – he was level-headed and had no time for the supernatural. If anyone of his acquaintance admitted to having seen a spook, Henry would laugh him out of the room. However, all that was to change.

One winter's evening in 1917, Henry, a Sergeant in a northern regiment, was hurrying down Westgate Road in Newcastle, where he owned a trim little home. He was groping his way towards Newcastle Central station through a particularly thick, acrid fog that had descended like a blanket over the area. He had nearly lost his bearings when a voice came to him out of the gloom.

'Are you lost, mate?'

Henry gasped in surprise. 'I want to go to Central station,' he replied.

'That's all right,' replied the voice. 'I'm going there myself – keep close and we'll get there somehow.'

Henry gratefully fell in beside the stranger who had now emerged out of the fog. Westgate Road was very quiet, the sounds from the industrial premises seemed strangely muted, and the air was damp and cold, penetrating the clothing. The fog was acrid and made talking somewhat painful, so the two men did not try to converse.

As they passed through pools of light carved into the fog by the hissing gas lamps, Henry Kirkup took a glance at his companion, who was now revealed by his flashes to be a Sergeant in a southern regiment. Henry noticed, however, that the soldier's uniform was of a kind worn in the South African War some 16 years earlier. Henry was just going to ask the other why he was wearing such an outdated uniform when the stranger spoke.

'Are you going back to your unit?'

Henry said that he was.

'So am I,' said the other. 'I have to catch a train from here to London.'

'I too,' said Henry. 'We could travel together, for company of course.'

'Certainly,' replied the other. 'I'll be pleased to have someone to talk to.'

On arrival at Newcastle Central they found the train waiting, and soon settled in an empty compartment. By this time the fog was beginning to clear and Henry could see one or two stars glowing faintly in the winter sky.

'This night is similar to one night in 1899. I will never forget it,' the stranger remarked.

Henry was interested. 'A long time to remember 1899!'

'I have very good reason to remember it,' said the South African Sergeant. He blew his nose. 'I'll tell you about it. I was pleased with myself that night. I had found an empty compartment and I settled down to doze a little; then a man got in and sat down opposite me looking at me in a shifty way. He looked mean, and ill at ease, but I was tired – I'd done a hard day's work recruiting for the regiment in Newcastle.

'I felt in my pocket for a cigarette and accidentally pulled out my wallet and my pay packet, which spilled out on to the floor. I picked it all up but the other man was watching me intently like a dog watches a rabbit. I was almost dropping off to sleep with fatigue when the man leapt up and made a lunge at me. He had a long knife. I grabbed his wrist and deflected the blade of the knife, whereupon we both rolled about on the floor.'

Henry asked, 'Did you win the fight?'

'No,' said the stranger. 'Although my attacker was very thin he was stronger than me and as I tried to reach the window communicating cord he pulled me back and plunged the knife into my chest.'

'But were you lucky? Did you deflect the blade into a less vulnerable spot?' asked Henry, feeling slightly sick at the gruesome description of the fight.

'No,' said the other, 'I was unlucky. He did not miss, he killed me.'

'He did what?' gasped Henry, looking across the compartment. He couldn't believe his eyes. The stranger had gone, dissolved into thin air. Henry was on his own in the compartment as the train drew further and further away from Newcastle.

28
The visitor

*I*can think of no more bizarre situation than going into a platelayer's hut to have a snack and sitting quite comfortably munching away, only to have a ghost walk in, move to the far corner and stand gazing into the dark recesses. Such was the experience of my correspondent Mr C. Whitehead, who kindly sent me his memories of the startling event.

The story begins in the late 1950s when Mr Whitehead was employed by British Railways as a platelayer on the main line between Ramsbottom and Helmshore. Shortly before he took up the job, two members of the gang had been having a go at each other; niggling at first, their relationship became strained and matters were getting worse. Soon the two men were nearly at one another's throats and it took the others in the gang to keep them apart.

One day one of the gang was walking the length, looking at the condition of the track and the fishplates, checking for possible broken rails and pumping ballast, when he came across a platelayers' cabin with the door open; fearing that the cabin had been broken into and the tools stolen, he ventured inside. He had hardly passed through the door when he was killed by a vicious blow from an axe wielded by one of the quarrelling men. He had killed the wrong man! From then on the cabin was known as 'The Murder Cabin'.

It was some time later that Mr Whitehead came across the spectre of the murdered man; he had already made his presence known to several permanent way workers, who had nicknamed him 'George'. The weather had been threatening rain, and when the heavens opened Mr Whitehead had to run for cover. Seeing the cabin nearby he raced to it and sought shelter; it was dark in the small building but it was dry and it served its purpose.

He had not been there long when a shadow fell across the door. A man walked in, went over to the far corner and stood silently. Mr Whitehead shivered. It had suddenly turned quite cold, and the rain was still coming down fast. The stranger did not move, and Mr Whitehead did not feel menaced by his presence, so sat still and waited for the rain to stop. Eventually it did and the sun came out, and Mr Whitehead got up and walked out into the fresh air. The stranger followed him and disappeared like a puff of smoke. Our friend could not believe his eyes.

Some weeks later the whole gang was squeezed into one of the cabins to shelter from the elements. The air was thick with smoke and the earthy smell of human beings crushed together. Then the door opened and in walked 'George'. He glided through the men to the far corner and stood in his usual posture gazing into the darkness. Mr Whitehead then told the foreman of his own experience with 'George'. The foreman did not laugh or pour scorn on Mr Whitehead's revelation; he just said, 'Don't worry, he won't hurt you. He often comes in to see us.'

I understand that his murderer was caught and paid the ultimate penalty for this dreadful crime. Today the track and other infrastructure has been removed between Ramsbottom and Helmshore, and so too have the old platelayers' cabins. But I wonder if 'George' still wanders about looking for the huts that he used to frequent in search of his old workmates. . .

29
Ghosts at Kidlington

On Christmas Eve 1874 a GWR Paddington-Birkenhead train packed with people returning home for the seasonal festivities was derailed near Shipton-on-Cherwell, Oxfordshire, following the breakage of a tyre on one of the carriages. Nine carriages left the track and plunged down a steep embankment into the Oxford Canal. Thirty-four people died in the crash and resultant fire, and over 100 were injured in the worst disaster ever to occur on the Great Western Railway.

Since that time a remarkable series of events has taken place in a modern terraced house at the Moor, Kidlington, less than a mile from the scene of the tragedy. Ask Mr Brian Beck if he believes in ghosts. Mr Beck lives at the Moor, and he will answer, 'I haven't any choice, have I? It isn't imagination when you're lying in bed and you suddenly see the figure of a child move across the room and disappear through a closed door.'

Many other things have happened in the Becks' house: babies are heard crying, a poltergeist is very active moving things about, lights go on and off, doors open and shut on their own, sounds of footsteps are heard all over the house. At a Tupperware party held in the house, several ladies were astonished when scratching and tapping noises were heard to come from a glass-topped coffee table. One lady had to be taken home in a very distressed state, swearing that she would never enter the house again.

Mr Beck has been visited by the ghost of a lady who materialises in solid form – no haze or mist, but absolutely life-

like. Her visits are nocturnal and she arrives through the closed
door and approaches the bed; on one occasion Mr Beck awoke to
find this lady, dressed in black and with a very sorrowful face,
peering at him. Again, when Mr Beck was reading in bed one
night the lady appeared and put out the light. Mr Beck describes
her as under 40, dressed in black, her hair done up in a bun, or
tied neatly back under her bonnet; she seems to be around for
possibly 30 seconds to 1 minute. Mr Beck does not feel very
scared, more curious to find out her identity; but she disappears
as mysteriously as she arrives.

Mrs Beck describes an incident concerning her son Kye, only
2½ years old at the time, and certainly not able to use a pen. He
surprised his parents by drawing a star of David in a neat and
steady hand. He often said to his mother, 'I can't get to sleep –
please tell the children to leave the toys alone.'

A neighbour has gone on record as seeing a woman and two
children, followed by a man, walking towards the house, up the
garden path then just disappearing. 'Cold' spots are noted in
the house, while one spot near the bathroom has a strong smell
of ripe apples, and other smells are of burning ashes and
cooking – but not of this world! In the crash the coaches caught
fire – they were wooden and lit by gas – so that might account
for the strong smell of burning. One peculiar event was the
morning Mrs Beck came down to find the gas cooker 'sparkling
clean'.

How do we relate this bizarre litany of events to the horror of
the train crash? Some of the victims of the accident were taken
to nearby Hampton Gay Paper Mill to await identification; an
artist from *The Illustrated London News*, in an issue dated January
1875, described the appalling scene:

'One instance I witnessed of heart-rending grief will remain
indelibly imposed on my mind. Among the dead lay a young and
handsome youth of about twenty-one awaiting identification.
Hearing the rustle of a lady's dress close by, my attention was
fixed on the lady who had just entered. She was anxiously
scanning the many bodies and in a moment singled out the
handsome features of the dead boy. She fell prostrate with grief
over the cold, white face of her son, raining kisses on his lips that

could never return her love. Beside her was the father sobbing uncontrollably, silently watched by a policeman.'

How does the drawing of the woman made by the artist shortly after the accident compare with Mr Beck's nocturnal visitor? Mr Beck says there is a striking resemblance and the expression on her face is always the same; but why does she always come to this house when the crash happened nearly a mile away all those years ago?

The Becks have decided to continue to live with the phenomena and do not intend to move. A family who lived in the house previously also heard strange noises and heavy distinct footsteps in a bedroom. They didn't stay. . .

It would seem that the paranormal events are tied in closely with the train crash, and the lady in black is still looking for her son. Is it possible that some of the victims might have been taken to a building on the site of Mr Beck's house? One must admire the courage and resilience of the family that will not allow a supernatural force to drive them from their home.

30
Gas lamps and ghosts

*I*t was a dark night in November 1981 on the preserved Keighley & Worth Valley Railway, and the crossing keeper at Damens station was waiting for the passage of the last down train from Keighley. The station stood empty, and a light covering of frost lay illuminated by the incandescent glow from the gas lamps on the platform. Inside the signal box the gas lights were also lit and the fire in the pot-bellied stove was glowing red hot.

The keeper looked across at the empty station house; there was no one stopping there tonight. It was often empty now, Annie having left after her husband Norman died last Christmas; the nearest life was the main Halifax road about half a mile up the hill. What a lonely outpost! At least he had already brought in the lamp from the up home signal. He just had to see the last train up the hill, then lock the gates, bring in the gate lamps and the down home lamp, lock up the signal box, and go home.

Where was the train? It should have left Keighley 5 minutes ago. The clock ticked away, ever so slowly, it seemed. From his couch in the box the crossing keeper glanced up the line towards the loop; he couldn't see the loop box from the cutting, just the wires of the loop's down starter signals, and his own reflection in the glass – but what was the shadow behind him looking into the box?

He froze. At least the door was bolted, and the shadowy figure moved off down the platform, or so it seemed from the reflection. The man pulled himself together and dashed out of the door. 'Who's there?'

He expecting to hear one of the local gypsy lads running off, but there was not a sound. A shiver shot down his back; he lit a cigarette and went back into the box, bolted the door and sat down again. Where was that train?

He looked up the line again, but all he saw was his reflection – then that shadowy figure again. It was clearer this time and appeared to be wearing some sort of railway uniform. It certainly had a peaked cap, but no visible face! The keeper spun round and dashed outside straight away – but again there was not a sound, no one was there, just an uncanny silence. The river was silent, as was the little stream at the end of the platform; even the normally busy main road was quiet now.

What was that? A loud shriek told him that the Midland '4F' had whistled for the foot crossing – the train was here at last. The staff at Keighley must have been eager to get home as they hadn't phoned. The man darted to the crossing and opened the gates, pulling off the down home signal just in time. The train stormed through the tiny station unaware of the goings on there, and he belled it on to the next station.

He then closed the crossing gates and was up and down the signal like a cat after a bird. He pulled down the shutters, turned off the gas, locked the door and dashed off home. Had the gas lamps been playing tricks? Or one of the gypsies? Or had it really been a ghost? Whatever it was, he took steps to make sure that he was not there alone at night from that day to this!

31
The man in the mist

*I*f one is to believe statistics, only 2 per cent of the world's population are gifted with 'second sight' or the ability to witness paranormal phenomena, but how many of these fortunate or unfortunate people ever realise this power? It will manifest itself maybe once in their lifetime, often leaving horrific memories of their experiences.

The following story is an example of an incident that left an indelible mark in my correspondent's memory. Mr Alistair Robertson was returning to his home in Edinburgh after a business trip to London. On arriving at King's Cross he found a seat in an open coach, put his case on the luggage rack and settled himself down for a good read. The coach was quite full with the usual business executives chatting away. Alistair had made the journey many times and thought he knew every mile of the journey intimately.

He had bought a paperback at the station bookstall; it was a war story and certainly nothing to do with the supernatural, so after reading the daily paper he started on his new book. At this stage I must inform the reader that Alistair Robertson did not tell anyone of his horrific experience for many years.

The coach was alive with the usual hum of conversation and noise, not intrusive but rather soporific, and Alistair began to nod off. He felt himself falling asleep and shook himself; he opened the ventilator and the breeze was most refreshing. After a while he closed the ventilator and read some more of his book.

After about an hour and a half the train entered a long tunnel.

Alistair was reading his book and was somewhat annoyed to discover that the carriage lights were not on, so he put down his book and waited for daylight to return.

But then a very strange thing happened. He was suddenly aware of what appeared to a mist forming over the seat opposite him. This puzzled him, as it was absolutely pitch black in the carriage. He thought at first that it must be steam drifting in from the steam heating system, but he lifted his hand to his face to find that he could not see it. He looked at the mist again and it began to swirl about, but still over the table in front of him and the seat opposite.

Alistair was becoming mesmerised by the strange experience; the mist was gradually resolving itself into the shape of an oldish man, nearly bald but well dressed in a well-cut city suit, somewhat redolent of a bank manager or some other business executive, definitely respectable. He was apparently a happy man because he was smiling. From his face he was about 55 years old, fairly plump, but everything about him seemed absolutely normal; it was just the way he had appeared that was so dramatic. The mist continued to swirl about him, mesmerising Alistair who was wide-eyed with surprise.

The man just sat and smiled, and Alistair noticed that amid the swirling mist behind the newcomer there appeared to be a window, and through it he could see a crowd of people milling about. They appeared to be moaning and wailing as if in great distress. But the man still smiled at Alistair, putting his hands on the table that separated them and leaning towards him. The fixed smile now became rather sinister, and began to assume grotesque proportions. He seemed to be rising out of the seat and coming closer and closer to Alistair, who was now terrified and was trying to force himself back into his seat. The man's leering face was moving still closer, and there seemed nothing to stop it, this nightmare. . .

Alistair then thought about the other people in the carriage who were so close but so far away; the puzzling thing was that he could not see them or even hear them, which did not exactly help his failing courage. As the man's face grew closer, Alistair could even feel his breath, or thought that he could.

Summoning up the remains of his courage, Alistair thrust his hand outwards at the face to ward it off, but to his surprise he touched nothing. The man leaned back and continued to smile that sinister, menacing leer. . .

Then to Alistair's relief the swirling mist began gradually to dissipate, reducing the man's shape to a vague outline. Alistair shook himself, bewildered by the whole sequence of events. Eventually the mist cleared completely and the man and the crowd of people behind him disappeared, the sounds of conversation of his fellow travellers returned, he could hear again the comforting sound of the rail joints, and normality was restored.

Alistair stood up and stretched, yawned, and looked out of the window. The passing countryside seemed so reassuring. He puzzled and gazed at the empty seat opposite. There was nothing to be seen at all. The two men sitting across the gangway were chatting happily, and all seemed normal, but who was the man? And why did he appear? These questions are still unanswered and perhaps always will be. . .

32
The man in the black beret

*T*his story concerns a young man who witnessed the replay of a past accident, seeing in graphic detail the appalling event. Andy had just left school and at the time of the incident, the 1960s, he was able to find a job with British Railways as an apprentice signalman. However, his first duties saw him engaged in the removal of redundant signalling equipment as part of the updating and modernisation of post-war British Railways.

Andy was working with two mates, Alf and Ron, who were older and much more experienced and were able to instruct Andy in the initial part of his training. This particular day was quite bright for December, and the three men enjoyed the 10-mile journey to the location where they had to dismantle a redundant signal cabin. The senior man, Alf, instructed Andy to remove the levers from the frame and load them into the BR van.

At about 3pm Alf asked Andy if he would walk to the nearby village and get them some cigarettes and chocolate as the men wanted a break. Andy set off along the deserted, rusting track, which was by now being covered by the spread of weeds and other undergrowth. Having made his purchases he started to walk back along the old railway line, this time walking on the sleepers. It was beginning to get dusk and the clouds were hastening the end of a winter's day.

He was about halfway back when he heard a noise that made his hair stand on end – the sound of a steam engine. Was it possible? He looked round, but there was nothing in sight; then faintly on the slight breeze he heard it again, the unmistakable sound of a steam engine, and it was approaching. Andy knew that steam motive power had ceased in that area many years before; anyway, the line had been closed to all traffic for months, so what was such an engine doing on the line now? He quickened his pace, knowing that something was wrong and wanting to get as far away from the place as possible. Panic set in when the sound of the engine became much louder, then he stumbled on the sleepers and fell face down. The engine was now almost upon him – he turned to look and an amazing sequence of events unfolded before his eyes.

The whole area was bathed in a haze of yellow light that seemed somehow menacing. He tried to get to his feet but for some reason was unable to do so. He heard the bloodcurdling shriek of the engine's whistle, its piercing note splitting the December air. Then Andy saw the tall figure of a man dressed in railway uniform and wearing a black beret, like those worn by the Royal Tank Corps, instead of the regulation railway hat. The figure stood in the track seemingly rooted to the spot and made no move to avoid the oncoming engine. Finally there was a horrible piercing scream from the figure as the engine struck it and ground it beneath its wheels.

At last Andy found his feet and ran as fast as he could back to the other men; he leapt through the door of the box and collapsed on the floor. When Alf had revived him with a cup of strong tea he poured out his story.

'Don't be daft,' they scoffed:

'I tell you I saw him killed,' gasped Andy, 'and he was wearing a black beret like the Tank Corps wear.'

Alf stroked his chin. 'A black beret?' Then the recollections came flooding back and Alf told Andy the story. 'I remember now. About nine or ten years ago there was a bloke killed doing track maintenance work around here – he wore a black beret and was well known. I think he had been in the Tank Corps or something like that, but you wouldn't know anything about that, would you?'

Andy replied, laughing, that it was a bit before his time, and without further ado they loaded the van and left, vowing never to return to the area again; another gang finished the job.

As far as is known there has been no further sighting of the phantom engine. Andy is now happily married with two fine children and when they ask about ghosts Andy shakes his head.

33
The revenge of the old soldier

*T*he type of supernatural phenomenon that returns to wreak revenge for an earthly feud is fortunately in the minority, but ghosts that kill are still evident in certain circumstances.

Tom Howe was an engine driver. He was also a highly skilled engineer and in his youth had been apprenticed to a firm of railway engineers at Doncaster. He was a burly, well-built man, liked by his workmates; he had a practical disposition and he certainly did not believe in ghosts or the supernatural.

In 1901 he moved to London and set up home with his family near King's Cross station. Later that year he met an old friend, Len Curtis, with whom he had worked at Doncaster. Len had moved to London earlier, so it was a happy reunion. Eventually Howe became fireman to Curtis on the night expresses to the North.

When the First World War began the two men served together in the 42nd Division at Gallipoli. When peace returned they again worked together in the same link. Len married and Tom was his best man, but unknown to both men this was where the trouble began that was to end their friendship. The two families became very friendly and visited each other's homes regularly, and Tom became very fond of Ellen Curtis, who was 15 years younger than her husband.

Tom Howe eventually became a driver himself and his duties would often take him past the Curtis home at Finsbury Park; whenever he had any spare time he would visit Ellen, telling his own wife that he had business elsewhere. Eventually Ellen had a baby, and local rumour had it that Tom was the father.

Then news of Tom's interest in his wife reached Len Curtis, who was beside himself with fury; when he next met Tom he pulled him out of the cab of his loco and warned him not to see his wife again. The next day Tom was transferred to the early morning express to Newcastle via York, but the train was on the same line that ran past the Curtis home and unknown to her husband Ellen used to wave to Tom as he passed, and on the homeward run she would wave an oil lamp.

One wet Saturday night Tom noticed from the cab of his engine that Ellen's signal lamp was for the first time missing; he slowed down for the network of points near the Curtis home and whistled, but there was no sign of Ellen. As he cycled home from the shed he noticed a poster advertising the local paper: 'TRAGEDY IN RAILWAY COTTAGE. ENGINE DRIVER KILLS WIFE AND CHILD THEN COMMITS SUICIDE'. The following day Tom Howe found out that his former workmate and friend had indeed murdered his family, then killed himself.

Time passed by with its usual routine, and Tom always looked out of the cab when he reduced speed for the points and glanced at the cottage where the Curtis family had lived, more out of habit than morbid curiosity.

Then one night a horrific series of events occurred that was to cost Tom Howe his life. As usual he closed the regulator to slow down for the points, and leaned out of the cab to look for the cottage, when his fireman yelled at him with a terrified look on his face. His mate was pointing to the regulator, which was moving on its own into the open position.

The train was now gathering speed and approaching the points, and to his horror Tom saw th   ith of Len Curtis holding the regulator wide open; but the strange thing was that he was wearing the uniform of the 4?   he one he had worn at Gallipoli!

Tom made a grab for the handle to pull it back   ' ze speed, but he could not move it. He saw the ghostly figure disappear into the steam as the engine, by now completely out of control, hit the points at excessive speed, derailed and hit the embankment wall. Tom Howe was killed instantly, but the fireman survived to vow that the ghost of Len Curtis had indeed returned to wreak a terrible revenge.

34
The sealed tunnel

Nineteen-year-old Pamela Goodsell's eyes nearly left their sockets when she saw what the light of the match revealed. It was an old train, with the remains of passengers, now skeletal, lying in some disarray on the mouldering floor of the carriage, wearing Victorian-style clothing with some of the men sporting top hats. The train had apparently been sealed up in an underground tunnel, but why?

The teenager had fallen down a 20-foot shaft while walking through a park near the site of the old Crystal Palace in South East London. She was horrified by her discovery, yet of course very puzzled that the local authorities had not exhumed the remains and thus brought the train's existence to light. But when she made enquiries about her find, no one wanted to know.

'Completely preposterous', said London Transport. 'There is no record of a subway train crash in the area.' The spokesman went on to say that 'We just don't lose trains and passengers like that, not even in Victorian times.'

Miss Goodsell, who claims to have found the remains in 1978, could not, however, find the shaft when she went back to the park. But she remains quite unshakeable in her account of the horrific experience, and it seems that nearly all Sydenham knows that there is an abandoned underground train somewhere under the park, possibly the result of an experiment that went badly wrong. Legend has it that the train was shunted into a tunnel around 1870 and was never seen again, perhaps conveniently forgotten by the authorities who preferred to bury their mistake for ever.

One excuse put forward is that the relevant documents appertaining to the mystery were lost during the last war. However, experts have been successful in tracing the mystery back to an experimental train designed by an engineer named T. W. Rammell, which once ran for 600 yards on a line between Sydenham Gate and Penge. Compressed air was pumped into the tunnel, which was sealed with airtight doors, and the train careered along at about 35mph... No record of any accident was made, but the experiment was soon discontinued and no other prototype constructed; was the train sealed up in its tunnel and forgotten by the outside world?

Subsequently I understand that members of the London Underground Railway Society and the Norwood Historical Society showed a keen interest in the mystery. They obtained permission to sink boreholes in the park to identify the site of the tunnel, and special electronic tests were made, the intention being to uncover the whole train intact.

People in the area cannot explain the occasional rumblings that are sometimes heard at different times of the year. Are they connected with this dreadful accident? Can they be explained?

35
The wreck of the Scottish Mail

*W*hen driver Ben Fleetwood and fireman Jack Talbot reported for duty at 2 o'clock on the afternoon of 19 September 1906, they each had exactly 9 hours left to live. The manner of their dying was to leave behind what is probably the greatest unsolved mystery in British railway history.

Together they made a good, well-experienced and cheerful footplate crew. Fleetwood was a dignified, trusted, well-liked man of flawless character, and Talbot was a more than fully competent, well-trained main-line fireman. He was also a qualified driver and design engineer, and had been destined to be employed on the staff of the Chief Mechanical Engineer. If you were a passenger on a high-speed night express, here surely was a crew in which you could put your trust.

Their tour of duty for each day of this particular week was a straightforward job of three separate trips. After booking on at Doncaster shed, they worked the 3 o'clock afternoon passenger train to York. From York they worked the 6.50 express to Peterborough, and from Peterborough they worked the London-Edinburgh night mail back as far as Doncaster, where they were relieved and booked off duty. This was a rostered job in the express passenger link and therefore came round to each footplate crew regularly every few weeks. Certainly Fleetwood and Talbot had worked this particular duty many times.

The engine, an Ivatt 'Atlantic', was of a well-proven class and was virtually brand new – Jack Talbot, as part of his engineering apprenticeship, had helped to built it. Both men knew the route thoroughly, the locomotive was hauling a train well within its capabilities, the night was dark with occasional flurries of rain but visibility was excellent, and the train was running exactly to time and, until the approach to Grantham station, under clear signals – yet this footplate crew and 12 of their unsuspecting passengers were about to die.

At a few minutes before 11 the train was approaching Grantham, the only stop before Doncaster. On the platform at Grantham stood a station inspector and a small group of Post Office employees. They were preparing for quick action, for they had barely 2 minutes in which to haul almost a hundred mail bags into the mail vans of the train once it had stopped.

On this night it did not stop. The signalmen at each end of the station and the small group on the platform looked on in petrified disbelief and horror as the night mail thundered headlong into the station. Wreathed in steam and bathed in the crimson glow from the open firebox, the locomotive roared past the platform and disappeared out into the darkness at the north end of the station – then left the rails at the junction with the Nottingham line, where the points had been set for the branch to protect an incoming train.

It was a crash of appalling destruction, a holocaust of mangled timber and metal that soon became a funeral pyre. The crackle of the flames, the hiss of escaping steam, the shouts of arriving rescuers and the screams of the dying became a horrifying amalgam of tragic sound that stunned the senses of those running to help.

The locomotive was completely and utterly wrecked. Daylight revealed it as a tangled heap of twisted metal that could give no clue to the cause of the disaster. Neither could Fleetwood or Talbot. They had been killed instantly.

For all the light it threw on the matter the investigation might as well never have been held. This was no fault of the investigators. There was literally nothing to investigate, no objects to examine, no person to question and no papers to read. The night mail had stormed at high speed through Grantham station, raced out into the darkness – and crashed.

The stark simplicity of that statement says all that can really be said about this mystery. Various people offered a variety of improbable solutions, but no one explanation held much more water than any other. If there was a popular theory, it was simply that both men had forgotten where they were on the line. But Grantham was a busy, well-lit station and the two signal gantries guarding it from the south carried groups of signals that were totally unique to the location. Either man on the footplate could read this signal layout as easily as telling the time by the town hall clock. It was easily proved that they were both awake. The signalman at Grantham South had a clear view of the footplate and both enginemen were standing on their respective sides, the driver at the controls and the fireman standing close to the boiler front, as the train came storming into the station.

So the wreck of the Scottish Mail passed into railway legend and whatever happened on the footplate of the locomotive that tragic night none of us will ever know.

36
The Hexthorpe ghost

This story took place one dark night in late autumn a few years ago at the Cherry Tree sidings at Hexthorpe, a mile west of Doncaster. The sidings were in those days used mainly for coal and coal empties traffic, and it was while shunting empty coal wagons that the following incident took place. Let the engine driver himself recount the tale.

'My second man and myself were looking through the rear windows of our diesel locomotive awaiting a signal from the yard staff. After a minute or so the shunter signalled us with his lamp to proceed down the yard to attach a rake of wagons. As I turned to open the power controller on the loco I noticed the figure of a man coming across the adjoining tracks towards us. He appeared to be dressed in a light-coloured mackintosh and cap. I lowered the cab window and shouted, "Hey, where do you think you're going?"

He ignored my call and by now had reached the line on which we stood. Although I could clearly see his outline and had no doubt whatsoever that it was a man, I could not see his face or features, only his cap and a dark mask where his face would normally be. By now he had passed out of my sight at the rear of the loco. Turning to my second man I said, "Has that bloke come out clear on your side?"

"No, there's no one here," he replied.

At the same time we both climbed down the steps at either side of the loco and met at the rear. The man was nowhere to be seen. By now the shunter had walked up the siding to where we stood and asked what was wrong. I told him what had happened, and the three of us again searched all around the loco and the surrounding sidings, but to no avail. There was no sign of anyone.

The shunter said that he had heard of the ghost of a man sitting on the buffer stops at the end of the sidings, but thought that his mates were trying to frighten him. Now he was less sure.

Two weeks later I was in the signal box at St James Junction, at the opposite end of Hexthorpe yard from where the above sighting took place. I was waiting to conduct a Tinsley train crew into the Decoy marshalling yard at Doncaster. During my conversation with the signalman I mentioned the ghost. He was very startled and uneasy for a minute or so, then went on to tell me of what had happened the last time he had been on nights in that box.

He had a train of wagons bound for Wath-on-Dearne standing in his section and the brake-van was about 20 yards beyond the signal box. Everything was quiet when all of a sudden he heard someone shouting. Before he could get to the door of the box it burst open and in staggered a guard. According to the signalman the poor fellow was in such a state that he could neither stand nor speak.

"I sat him down and quickly made him a cup of tea. After a while the guard, who was in charge of the train outside the signal box, was able to tell what had happened. He had been sitting quietly in his brake-van waiting for the train to move off when the rear door of the van had opened and a man in a light raincoat had walked in and without saying a word had gone out of the other door without opening it – in other words he had walked through a closed door!"

It is obvious that this was the same ghost as the one I had seen two weeks earlier. Who he was or why he was there I don't know to this day, but I do know that he was there, and maybe still is.'

37
The letter

'Goodbye son,' said Mrs Ayscough, trying hard not to weep but yielding to nature and brushing a tear away with her glove.

'Goodbye mother . . . and don't worry. We shall all be home by Christmas. They've got the Kaiser on the run already. I doubt if they'll even need us.'

But his last words were drowned in a hiss of escaping steam and Mrs Ayscough waved and waved not only until had the train had vanished from view but also until everyone had left the platform.

'There, there, Mrs Ayscough. . .' It was Tom Farrow, the station master. 'Don't take on so. Your Bob'll be home before you know where you are.'

He put his arm gently round her shoulder and guided her to the station entrance. She went reluctantly and he watched her set off for her house down Station Road.

That night Mrs Ayscough said her prayers as she always did, but that night they were more fervent than usual. She tried to imagine Bob far away in France, translating him in her mind to a foreign field. But the field she conjured up bore a marked resemblance to the field next door to her house where Bob had played in his childhood.

She thought about her son every day, prayed for him every evening and looked forward to the first letter he had promised to write to her. But when the letter came it was not brought by the postman. Mr Farrow the station master brought it. It was a small letter, a letter in a brown envelope, an envelope without a stamp and with OHMS written upon it.

Mr Farrow stayed with her until she had read the letter's brief sentence, and he stayed with her until the light faded and she went to bed, alone, to pray and to drift into merciful sleep.

The following day Mrs Ayscough walked down the road to the railway station. She thanked Mr Farrow for his kindness and stood on the platform, gazing down the line, listening to the wind in the telegraph wires, looking at the silver ribbons of rail as they curved away into the cutting beyond the village. She came again the next day, and Mr Farrow watched from his office window as she stood alone, keeping a solitary vigil, staring into the distance.

She did it every day. And when, in November 1918, the war came to an end, she still did it. She walked to the station in all weathers, always alone, always at the same time, and stood for about 5 minutes transfixed.

In 1958, at the age of 80, Mrs Ayscough died. Two years later the village railway line was closed. For some time the railway station stood empty and deserted. The signals and the signboards were all removed, and one day the premises were bought and converted into a house.

Maureen and John Parker made an excellent job of the alterations and lived happily at Station House for many years. As newcomers they knew nothing of either Mr Farrow or of Mrs Ayscough, or of Mrs Ayscough's only son . . . until one night after Christmas in 1981.

It had been a bitterly cold day and that night a blizzard sprang up. The Parkers, snug indoors, were about to go to bed when simultaneously they both felt that they heard shouting outside. The noise of the storm was by this time so great that both doubted their own ears. But someone seemed to be calling 'Bob' and another voice seemed to reply 'Mother'.

They stood still in the hall at the foot of the stairs, listening, craning, then John stepped to the window and drew back the curtains. Looking out across the platform he thought he could discern the figure of an old lady, standing by the platform edge staring up what had been the railway track. And when he looked again there was another figure moving towards her, a man, a soldier in a peaked cap and carrying a slung rifle.

John motioned to his wife to join him, but when he looked back there was no one there, only drifting snow, piling up outside the door. Despite his wife's protests that he was on a fool's errand, he struggled into his coat and boots and strode out into the blizzard, along the edge of the platform.

There was not a soul in sight, nor were there voices or footprints in the snow, nor any living mortal thing. He returned to the house, closed the door behind him and took off his coat, shedding snow on the carpet. It was only when he took off his boots that he noticed the piece of brown paper sticking to the sole. Carefully he removed it and, brushing the snow from it, saw that it was an envelope, a small brown envelope, an envelope with the initials OHMS written upon it. And there was a letter in it, a letter just one line long, a line that began: 'Dear Mrs Ayscough, I regret to inform you. . .'

38
Sharpthorne Tunnel

I have visited many disused railway stations and have walked miles of former trackbed without experiencing any feelings other than sadness and loss. So far I have yet to experience a ghostly sound or sighting, but perhaps I am unlucky! Sometimes I wish that I could have the sense of being able to lift the veil like so many of my kind correspondents, but they tell me that I am lucky.

To some people, the ability to participate in a paranormal event seems so easy that it appears as if these people generate and possibly energise the sequence of events that result in a manifestation. Take the story of a friend of mine, a level-headed, no-nonsense disbeliever who had a traumatic experience in a disused tunnel in the south of England.

During the early 1960s my friend was spending some time around the Bluebell Line in rural, leafy Sussex when he decided to have a look at the sad removal of track and facilities at West Hoathly. This station is situated north of Horsted Keynes, which was then the northern terminal of the Bluebell Line, and Sharpthorne Tunnel is situated between the two. It was a Saturday and the workmen were having their weekend off, so the place was deserted.

The old station was a sad sight without any commuters to give it life. It stood empty, abandoned and left to rot until some unfeeling demolition firm would raze it to the ground. Everything was quiet and autumn leaves covered the ground, the now lifeless trackbed telling its own story. After examining the station my friend decided to walk down the trackbed to find the tunnel about which he had heard.

He walked into the cutting and saw the mouth of the tunnel ahead; it was a very straight tunnel and he could see the bright sunlight at the end of the bore. He decided to go in and explore; the track had been removed but the entrances had not been sealed. Consulting his notes, he discovered that the tunnel was nearly half a mile long. He ventured in, the sound of his footfalls on the ballast somewhat reassuring; he was conscious of the encroaching darkness as he progressed further.

Now and again he paused and looked back to the receding sight of the old station; then he looked ahead to the welcoming circle of sunlight at the other end of the tunnel. The sound of water dripping from the vaulted brick roof was rhythmic and evocative.

He had been progressing steadily for perhaps 10 minutes when he suddenly became aware of another presence in the tunnel. He stopped and listened, but only the drip of water, sometimes near at hand, sometimes distant, broke the silence.

Then my friend's hair rose on the back of his neck as a figure flitted from one side of the tunnel to the other, passing across the bright circle of sunlight. It was unmistakable, it happened, he saw it. It made no sound, which was strange as the ballast had echoed under my friend's footsteps.

The figure was now lost in the shadows of the tunnel. Was it hiding in a manhole? Or was it waiting in stealth to strike him? He stopped walking and peered into the stygian darkness. All manner of thoughts crowded his mind; what was the figure up to? Was it scavenging, or just some youth trying to frighten someone?

There was no sign of movement now and no light, which was strange as anyone searching in the corners of this tunnel would need some sort of illumination. At this stage my friend had not thought of the supernatural; besides, he did not believe in that sort of thing. . . He looked back to the station end of the tunnel; it seemed a long way away.

Since there was now no sign of the figure, he decided to go on a bit further, only to find that his legs would not move forward. He tried again, but it was as if an invisible barrier was holding him back. He was really afraid now, and he decided to beat a dignified retreat. He turned and walked slowly back, his legs working perfectly.

Just to reassure himself, he again turned round and tried to go the other way. He was doing well when all of a sudden he came up against the invisible barrier again. He picked up a piece of ballast and threw it, watching the stone disappear into the darkness. Then he ducked as he heard it hit something. It was no good, he would have to get out of the strange place – once in the daylight, common sense would return.

It seemed a long way back to the cutting and the station; he was sweating in his haste and sat down on a low wall to think things out. He had been taking photographs before he entered the tunnel and he was certain that he had not seen anyone else enter. Admittedly he had only had a brief glimpse of the figure, but it had made a lasting impression. Any other person would have betrayed their presence by the sound of their footfalls on the thick ballast on the tunnel floor.

As a matter of interest my friend has spoken to other people who have ventured into the depths of Sharpthorne Tunnel and they too have had a very strong feeling of being watched by something. The paranormal does indeed seem to have been at work, mystifying and tantalising mortals that have dared to venture into the damp gloom. Was the sinister figure a former casualty of some railway disaster who returns to the scene of the accident? So far no explanation has been offered.

39
The sinister suitcase

*T*his story concerns not a ghost, but a sinister mystery that was never resolved, with implications both horrific and unpleasant. The police in the 1920s did not have the forensic skills or facilities that they have today to help them in their task of bringing criminals to justice, news did not travel so fast, and life was certainly more relaxed, but of course determination and dedicated application to every problem was still the hallmark of police work.

The story was related to me some time ago, but the lady concerned does not wish to be identified, so let her tell it herself.

'The gas lamps flickered in the slight breeze that stirred the night air as I stood with my mother on the platform of Harrogate station on a dark and dismal night in the early 1920s. Suddenly out of the gloom a man appeared beside us carrying a large suitcase. His face was partly covered by a scarf and the upturned collar of his long black raincoat, and he wore a shapeless trilby hat that had seen better days.

"Are you waiting for the Leeds train?" he asked in a well-modulated but somewhat husky voice; my mother answered in the affirmative.

About 5 minutes later the tank engine hauling the Leeds train clanked into the station, wheezed to a halt and stood simmering. We climbed into a compartment occupied by a lady and gentleman, my mother put our modest luggage on the luggage rack and we settled down on the dusty seats. A porter came along slamming doors and calling 'All stations to Leeds', then the carriage door was opened and the man with the suitcase who had spoken to us appeared, thrust the suitcase at our feet and melted into the night.

My mother looked at the case, a puzzled frown on her face. "Does this case belong to you?" she asked the lady and gentleman.

They stared at us and shook their heads. "Why, isn't it yours?" the gentleman asked, surprised.

My mother replied that it had nothing to do with us, and glared at the large case as if it were an object of menace. The train started up, gathered speed and rattled into the night. The gentleman spoke up again.

"I say, what a strange turn-up. Fancy leaving a thing like that – perhaps someone is picking it up at Leeds. I'll tell the guard when we stop."

We all eyed the case with deepest suspicion as if it would suddenly open up and attack us. Then I swallowed my fear and tried to see through the dusty window, but all I could make out was the reflection of the others in the compartment.

Then the lady spoke. "There was something in the papers last week about a case being found at a railway station and later on when someone opened it they found a dismembered body inside . . . a human body."

I shuddered and moved closer to my mother, who pursed her lips and frowned. "What a thing to discuss. How horrible. I prefer not to think of such things."

We now all gazed at the case with horror. What if it contained a body or the remains of one? We moved our feet away as far as possible.

"We will be stopping at Pannal shortly; perhaps we can get rid of it there," suggested the gentleman. "I shall put it off there, I shall." He looked at us all and glared.

As the train drew into Pannal my mother lowered the window and called the porter. He looked amazed as mother told him the story, but to our relief he took the suitcase, somewhat gingerly, and departed. We all sighed, looked at each other, and smiled. Had we worried unnecessarily? Were we premature in our wild thoughts? As the worry slipped from our minds we spent the rest of the journey speculating on what might have been in the sinister suitcase. Did it contain a dismembered body? Or the proceeds of a robbery? Would we ever know?

At last the train drew into Leeds and came to a halt. My mother and I stepped out on to the platform, gathered our luggage and said goodbye to our travelling companions, then I turned to look up at the station clock. As I turned my head my eye caught a glimpse of a tall man in a black raincoat wearing a scarf, his collar turned up, a battered trilby pulled down over his eyes coming towards us clutching a large suitcase. . .'

40
The mystery of the sad lady

*I*am greatly indebted to Mr Gordon Nash of Aylesbury, Bucks, for his following detailed account of an incident on a London tube train in January 1983:

'I am a building surveyor by profession, and as a result of my work I have had occasion to visit a considerable number of places where one might expect to find things a little beyond the realms of human comprehension. I do find that some places and buildings have a "feel"; in most cases it is welcoming and homely, but sometimes the opposite will occur. Usually I put these feelings down to my own imagination, which has been influenced by memories of stories and yarns that could connect with a particular style of building or environment, but the strange thing about the incident with which we are concerned is that it took place in the heart of busy, dirty London, not in a lonely country house or remote country station.

Before 1982 most of my work had been in Buckinghamshire and Hertfordshire, but during that year my employers moved to Victoria in central London. As I had no wish to move into the capital, I became one of the faceless thousands who commute into London. Luckily I only had to go to the office two or three times a week, for the property owned by my employers was mostly in the Home Counties.

My journey to work involved catching a train from Aylesbury to Marylebone, then travelling by underground from there to Oxford Circus using the old Bakerloo Line. I then used to change trains at Oxford Circus, take a Victoria Line train down to Victoria, then walk to the office. For the most part the journey was very uninteresting.

I used to leave home early in the morning to catch the 7am train from Aylesbury, and the winter mornings were the worst, with the rain streaming down the dirty windows of the ageing DMU, and nothing to see except the blank expressions of my travelling companions. Once again I might have expected something unusual on this part of the journey, as it involves travelling over the old Metropolitan Railway that used to terminate at Verney Junction. The line was also once shared by the impressive Great Central Railway but, alas, the great days of the line had declined, and it was now merely a "cattle truck" commuter route designed to get as many people as possible into and out of London.

It was on one of those winter mornings during January 1983 that an event occurred that has left me wondering ever since. It was wet and very cold and dawn had just broken as the train pulled into Marylebone. I remember lingering for a while in the compartment to get my coat and briefcase as I had no real wish to dash out into the cold and wet. The day was going to be one of those gloomy, dark days that make everything in London take on the colour of cold, wet steel. I made my way to the southbound Bakerloo Line; most of the first rush of passengers had caught a previous train and I managed to get a seat on the ageing "rattler".

The trip to Oxford Circus was uneventful and, like many who use the underground, I switched off and gazed into nothingness. Changing from the southbound Bakerloo to the southbound Victoria at Oxford Circus was a shock in those days, as you stepped from the old red rolling-stock so familiar to those who knew the London underground during the 1930s and '40s into the 1970s world of silver trains and well-lit platforms.

However, still in my standard commuter daze, I got on to the southbound Victoria train, which was almost empty. I had selected a coach close to the front of the train because when it stopped at Victoria the exit to the main-line station was at the end of the platform near the driver's compartment. I relaxed slightly in the marginally more comfortable surroundings and as the train pulled out of Oxford Circus I took my paper from my case to finish reading an article that I had started on the main-line train.

We were gaining speed rapidly and the rocking motion made reading difficult, so I decided to survey my fellow passengers, which I often did to pass the time. I used to try to guess what they did for a living – just a quick glance so as not to cause any embarrassment. A banker? A clerk? I would never know, but it provided mild amusement to break the boredom.

On this occasion there were no more than a dozen people in the whole car. I had decided what one or two of them were when I was struck by a young woman sitting diagonally across the car from me, just the other side of the exit doors. She was wearing a full-length dark blue coat buttoned to the neck and on her lap was a large soft black handbag. However, it was not her dress that caused me to glance back at her, it was the expression on her face. She had dark hair tied back, dark eyes and attractive, slim features, but she looked ill. Her complexion was pale and there was very little colour in her cheeks; she had dark rings under her eyes and she stared into space as the train sped along. I looked back at my paper, not wanting to make her uneasy, but I could not take my mind off that sad but so beautiful face. Her expression mirrored the weather of the day – grey and overcast, imbued with deep despair.

As anyone who travels the Victoria Line will know, there is only one station between Oxford Circus and Victoria, and that is Green Park. I looked up again as the train pulled out of that station and noticed that the young lady was still seated in the same position. In fact, she did not appear to have moved a muscle, and the pallor remained, as did the look of despair. I turned back to my newspaper to overcome my feelings, which were beginning to reflect the young woman's appearance.

I felt the familiar braking of the train as we approached Victoria and heard the thunder of another train on the northbound line. At a point just before the station the northbound and southbound tunnels join in a single bore, and a train running in the opposite direction is often seen. This was always my signal to stand up and make my way to the doors. As I stood up I noticed that the sad young lady had left her seat, but she was not standing by the doorway closest to both of us. In fact, I was the only person in that doorway. I thought that perhaps I had distressed her with my glances and felt a little guilty.

I looked down the train towards the single door at the end of the car, expecting to see her standing near that exit. There were one or two people there but no sign of her. I was certain that no one had passed in front of me heading towards the rear of the compartment to use the other two sets of doors, but I looked anyway. Again, one or two people stood by the exits, but not the lady.

The train drew into the station and ground to a halt with the usual squeal of brakes and hiss of compressed air as the pneumatic doors rolled back. By now I was puzzled. Where had my strange travelling companion gone? I should add here that at no time during this strange sequence of events did I feel fear or unease. I looked up and down the platform just to satisfy my curiosity, but to no avail. It was not that the platform was crowded, but the few people who left the train did not seem to be in any hurry to reach street level and the cold winter air.

I even looked up and down the escalator as I ascended – nothing, other than the faceless crowd of which I normally formed part, and no sign of the pale young lady in the blue coat.

What I think now to be the truth began to dawn on me. Had I seen a ghost? But what would an apparition be doing on the 8.10am Victoria Line service southbound from Oxford Circus? Sometimes on cold winter's evenings when travelling home on the main-line train, watching the water droplets run down the dirt of the window and looking at my own grey reflection against the blackness behind the glass, I wonder who my ghost was and why she looked so much like a cold, grey, winter morning in London.

I have nothing to support my story, and I have nothing to gain by relating it. You may take it that it actually happened.'

41
The Midland brake-van

*I*t is not difficult to imagine weird and sometimes inexplicable 'happenings' and visitations in isolated places such as dark and wet railway tunnels, remote signal boxes lit only by flickering oil lamps throwing emotive shadows everywhere, or the gas-lit rural station, deserted yet atmospheric, the silent empty platforms seeming to recall passengers who have passed and are now part of the great unknown; even deep railway cuttings conjure up an aura of mystery.

It is of course only too true that some of these places have been the scene of tragic accidents, and echoes of the past often cling to scenes of tragedy. One such story concerns an unexplained 'visitation' that occurred in an old Midland Railway brake-van many years ago, shortly after the railway 'Grouping' of the early 1920s.

To those who have not experienced it, the interior of a brake-van at night, lit only by the guard's hand lamp and the intermittent flames from the open flap of the stove, could be so full of flickering shadows, emotive shapes and ethereal, mystical patterns as to perhaps unnerve even the most strong-willed creature.

The story of what happened to Immingham goods guard Edwin Carter one cold winter's night was told to me by his nephew Clive, who, on his retirement from South African Railways, where he had been employed as a freight foreman, was on a visit to his home town.

Uncle Edwin, Clive had to admit, was a bit of a character, and he had 'been around' a lot, but of all the stories he told, and there were many, the tale about this particular trip was one that he swore was true and totally unexplained. Even Clive was impressed by the seriousness of his old uncle's voice and demeanour when relating the happenings that night so many years ago.

However, let Clive tell the story, then we can make up our own minds.

'Uncle Edwin had signed on one night at 9.30pm at the Immingham empty sidings guards' room. Having been told where his train of coal empties stood, he opened his locker and took out his large leather bag and his hand lamp, then went outside and into the adjoining lamp room to trim his lamp. He then walked down his train to examine the couplings and to pick up any handbrakes that might have dropped down as the train was shunted. Reaching his brake-van he was pleased to see that it was a good GCR one and not one of those old rough-riding former Midland ones that were somehow still being used.

He lit his two side lamps and tail lamp, put some coal on the stove, which had been lit for him by the yard foreman, and walked back down the other side of the train to repeat his examination. He did not have to wait long at the head of the train for the arrival of the train engine, and as it reversed carefully he watched it buffer up, then removed the engine tail lamp to save the fireman the job. As he climbed up the steps to the footplate the driver greeted him.

"Hello, Edwin, how many have we got on tonight?"

"Only 35," he replied.

The fireman offered him a cup of tea from his brew can, which Edwin accepted gratefully.

"Whistle up when you're ready, Fred,' he said to the driver. "Draw up when the 'peg' comes off and I'll get in."

Minutes later he was in the brake-van and they were on their way. It was an uneventful trip to Stainforth, where they arrived and were relieved on time. In the old converted carriage messroom in the sidings they joined other train crews waiting their turn to work home. After about an hour Edwin was told that their train was next up and would be arriving in minutes, so they gathered up their things and went outside to wait.

They did not have long to wait and as their train came into view, headed by one of the splendid ex-GCR 2-8-0 "Supers", Edwin proceeded to walk down the line past the oncoming wagons to relieve the guard. The coal train came slowly past and he looked up to see to his disgust that the brake was one of the detested ex-Midland Railway "rough-riders". Edwin stood waiting for it to approach and come to a stand. He saw the train guard clamber down and greet him.

"Hello, mate! You've got 30 on for West Marsh, a single load, but you're in for a rough trip – the bloody thing rocks and rolls all over the place and it is cold and draughty, although I've tried to build the fire up for you."

Edwin climbed up into the brake and went inside. There was a huddled-up figure opposite the guard's seat adjacent to the big brake wheel. Whoever it was was evidently asleep, and Edwin thought it unusual that the other guard had not mentioned that he would have company for the ride. After all, it was nothing very strange for train crews to ride home in the brakes on occasions. However, he was not too bothered and went outside on the verandah to wait for the driver to whistle up to signal their departure.

On hearing the whistle he held his hand lamp out and waited for the acknowledging whistle blast, then went back inside the brake, sitting down on his seat opposite his travelling companion.

He could see little of the man in the dim interior, but could make out a uniform coat and a shiny peaked cap. Passing Thorne North, Edwin decided not to disturb him until they got to Gunness – he might be a Scunthorpe guard. He went through his usual routine, going outside on the verandah to look at the train to see if there was anything untoward such as signs of hot axle-boxes, but apart from the odd spark of a swinging brake block here and there coming into contact with a wheel, which was quite normal, everything was in order.

Going back inside the brake, he was about to sit down for a few minutes' "shut-eye" when he noticed with a shock that he was alone – his travelling companion had gone. Whatever had happened? The brake-van's front door was still secured, with a wedge under the door bottom to make it fast in the door frame, so he could not have gone out that way. Edwin began to have doubts. Had the man existed? Could it have been a trick of the shadows? Had he imagined it? He thought hard. He had seen the uniform and the shiny cap – the figure had been real all right.

For the rest of the journey, despite being bounced and banged by the corkscrew motion of the brake, Edwin could not take his mind off the experience. A rational man, he did not like mysteries; to him everything was black or white, there were no grey areas of vague unexplained theory.

He looked hard at the seat on the other side of the brake that his companion had occupied and he willed the "ghost" or whatever it was to materialise again, but nothing happened. "As if it would," he thought. "I must be getting old or prematurely senile; perhaps I have been dreaming." The crowding thoughts took his mind off everything until with a lurch he realised that they had arrived at West Marsh sidings and he would now leave the old brake-van with its inexplicable presence to someone else.

When the train came to a halt he wound down the brake wheel and climbed down on to the ballast. He walked down the train to the engine and uncoupled between the tender and train, then clambered up on to the footplate.

"Had a good ride, Edwin?" asked the driver.

Edwin grimaced. "Rotten – not your fault, though. I was shaken up and banged about but I've arrived here in one lump so I can't grumble too much. But I'll tell you this, I never want to see that brake again. I've got its number and I'll take good care that I'll never ride in it again." He decided not to tell the driver and fireman about the queer figure because he would only get his leg pulled.

As he left to go home he could not resist going to have a look at the old Midland brake-van again. The moon had appeared from behind scudding clouds, briefly illuminating the scene, and the solidness of the van seemed curiously ominous as he approached. Then he spotted something. He stopped in his tracks and his mouth fell open. There on the verandah was a dark figure. It was in the shadow of the verandah's overhang, but it was there.

Edwin ran forward, convinced that someone was having a

joke, but as he got nearer to his amazement the figure melted into the night and the moon was again obscured by the night clouds.

About a year later, when talking to a Stainforth guard, he mentioned the experience. The guard had also seen the mysterious "passenger" on one occasion, and it was assumed to be the ghost of a guard who had died in the brake-van some years earlier while travelling home. Evidently the Stainforth men knew all about the apparition, and were not unduly concerned about the phantom passenger who travelled home with an earthly colleague.'

42
The phantom 'Western'

I am grateful to Mr G. Heathcliffe of Swindon for his account of the baffling reappearance of a 'Western' Class diesel-hydraulic locomotive, which was seen again after its demise at the hands of the dismantlers at Swindon Works.

Mr Heathcliffe is a railwayman. I suppose he could be referred to as a devoted 'Western' diehard, his main love during their reign being these 'Western' Class locomotives, which dominated express services from 1961 until the mid-1970s. His favourite loco in the class was D1042 *Western Princess*, and he was very disappointed when he was told that she was being withdrawn from service in July 1973 and was scheduled to be cut up in January 1974.

British Rail was rationalising its motive power and the diesel-hydraulic locos such as the 'Western' and 'Hymek' classes were to be withdrawn as the stock of spare parts became increasingly difficult to obtain. Another reason may have been that the availability of such locomotives was uneven, and the proposed new image of the 'supertrains', the HST 125s, and the electrification of many lines added to the demise of the hydraulics; ultimately the East Coast Main Line 'Deltic' diesel-electrics would share the same fate.

Mr Heathcliffe went with his father to Newbury races on a cold but sunny day in mid-May 1974. Mr Heathcliffe junior did not particularly like horses but the racecourse at Newbury was situated very near the main railway line to the West of England, so he thought he would see something interesting during the day out. However, during the first hour of watching the line only Class 47 locomotives were in charge of the trains to and from

Paddington, but eventually the unmistakable sound and shape of a 'Western' came into view. He could clearly see the number and name – it was D1041 *Western Prince* hauling well-filled coaches, and it was in good fettle, doing about 80mph. Following the train down he saw the blue sky darken and heard again the familiar 'Maybach music' (as the noise of the 'Western' Class engines is known to enthusiasts). Another 'Western' was approaching. From round the curve it came, highly polished and singing sweetly as only a well-maintained machine can.

As she drew level with him he could read very clearly the name and number – it was *Western Princess*, D1042. Deep joy! His favourite engine had been reprieved and repaired. This was not unknown on BR; withdrawn locomotives were sometimes taken out of store, overhauled and put back into service, mainly due to shortage of motive power.

However, a few days later a friend in Swindon Works said, 'I've got bad news for you. We cut up your old friend *Princess* on the 18th.'

'Oh no you didn't,' replied Mr Heathcliffe. 'I saw her on an up express at Newbury that day, so pull the other one.'

His friend persisted, but it was not until Mr Heathcliffe saw it in print that he actually believed that *Western Princess* was no more.

So what did he see at Newbury on 18 May 1974? He repeats that, as a railwayman, he knew what the locomotive looked like, even if he is a railway enthusiast! The shape and sound of a Maybach-engined 'Western' is unique and the only other 'Western' it could have been was *Western Prince*, and that had been seen moments before going in the other direction. Could he have witnessed the final fling of *Western Princess* on the day she 'died' in Swindon Works?

A similar experience was witnessed by a colleague one Saturday night in South Devon. He was heading east on an express between Plymouth and Totnes when it was stopped by engineering work. The locomotive on the engineers' train was D1067 *Western Druid*. Records show that this locomotive was cut up on 16 September 1976, yet the sighting in question was noted in February 1977.

So what can we deduce from these experiences? Mr Heathcliffe is adamant that his story is factual and completely without fabrication. Maybe the sceptics will smile, but those who understand such remarkable events will also smile – with contentment.

43
'Runaway trucks!'

Mr E. L. Anderson recalls an incident during the last war when he was in the RAF, stationed in Lincolnshire, as he travelled up by train from his home near Bedford.

One foggy Sunday night in February he caught a late train from an almost deserted Bedford station. As is sometimes the case when one embarks from a dark lonely platform, he had the feeling as the train wound its way through the flat fog-shrouded countryside that he was the only one aboard. After gazing out of the misty, dirty windows of the compartment for a while he snuggled down in his greatcoat and dozed off to sleep. The train normally took several hours to reach Lincoln, stopping and starting at frequent intervals, although nobody seemed to get on or off and no one joined him in his compartment.

Then suddenly the train came to a halt with a jolt that awakened him immediately and nearly deposited him on the carriage floor. He looked around, but he was still alone in the compartment. He could hear steam blowing off from the engine. Rubbing the misty window he peered through it, but could make out very little in the darkness outside. Plainly, though, they were nowhere near a station.

He sat for a while wondering what could have caused the sudden halt, then, pulling the strap that released the window, he slid it down. Putting his head out he gazed up and down the track, but could see nothing but fog-bound fields and a few lighted windows of the train he was in. Obviously he was not the only passenger aboard, but nobody else seemed to be taking any notice of the stoppage.

Then he heard the crunch of running footsteps and a man appeared out of the fog near the front of the train. As he approached, Mr Anderson could see that he was wearing what looked like the dark uniform of a railwayman and was waving his arms about. He was also shouting something, although it was not easy to make out what he was saying. Then, as he drew near, his words came clear. 'Runaway trucks!' he was shouting in a hoarse voice. 'Runaway trucks!' Then he had gone by and was running towards the rear of the train, soon disappearing into the fog.

Almost immediately the train jerked into motion and continued its slow progress. Mr Anderson sat back in his seat, nonplussed. Why had the train stopped suddenly, and just as suddenly started again? And who was the man running by the side of the track? What did he mean? Was there some danger? But nobody seemed bothered. The driver of the train was obviously proceeding, albeit at a slow pace, apparently unconcerned by the running man. But there was nothing that Mr Anderson could do. He was in a compartment on his own, in a non-corridor train, unable to communicate with anybody.

The train arrived at Lincoln without further incident. A few people got out, mostly service personnel, and went in search of the RAF lorries lined up in the station yard, which would take them to their respective camps in the county. Mr Anderson, still puzzled about what he had seen, joined them.

As he climbed aboard his own lorry he saw a group of friends. It appeared that they had been travelling on the same train, although he had not seen them. They had also noticed the train stopping abruptly, and although one or two had looked out, none had seen the running railwayman or heard the shouted words.

Mr Anderson later made enquiries of all airmen he could find who had travelled on the train that night and discovered that he was the only one who had seen and heard the running man. After thinking about it for some time he eventually decided that he must have been half asleep when the train shuddered to a halt and imagined the rest of the incident.

Years later, however, he read a newspaper account of some trucks that had broken free in a siding on the same line and smashed into a train coming the other way, killing the driver. Could he have witnessed something that was to happen in the future?

44
The footsteps on platform 4

*M*y correspondent, Mr R. L. P. Belanger, tells me a story about a mysterious phenomenon at Purley Oaks station in Surrey.

'Between 1962 and 1964 I was the leading porter at Purley Oaks station between Purley and East Croydon on the main line to Brighton, although we only had local trains stopping there.

In November 1963 the Oaks was still lit by gas lamps, which hissed and spluttered during the evening. To avoid hanging about after the last train departed we had worked out a system for closing down that went like this. The last Coulsdon North to Victoria train went at 10.45, so all lights on platform 1 were put out. At 11.08, when the last Caterham to Charing Cross train left, the lights on platform 3 and the end lights on 2 and 3 were put out and the booking hall was locked up. All tickets that had been collected were booked and the staff room was tidied up ready to lock up. The last Victoria to Coulsdon North train arrived at about 11.50, and the remainder of the island platform lights were put out, after which I returned to the staff room and locked up before meeting the last train. At 12.05 I crossed the station to deal with the last train, the 12.08 (if I remember correctly) from Charing Cross to Tattenham Corner, Caterham, an eight-car train. Purley Oaks platform 4 was built for three-car sets and only took six coaches, so the leading porter had to stand at the London end, to make sure that there were no passengers for the Oaks.

On the occasion in question nobody alighted, so, after giving the "all clear" to the guard, the train left. I then proceeded with my pole to put out the remaining lights, three at each end and two under the canopy and the waiting room. After putting out the London end and the canopy and waiting room, I started on the last three, walking towards the signal. After putting out the first light I heard footsteps on the stairs that led from the subway to the platform. Having to return that way I ignored them until, between the last two lights, with the footsteps getting closer, I turned round to offer whoever it was a lift into Purley. There was nobody there, yet the footsteps kept on coming towards me.

I turned and fled across four lines, looking neither left nor right. I threw my helmet on my head, put my greatcoat on the seat of my scooter and ran with it until it started, jumped on and was gone, leaving stairway and subway lights still on. I do not know who or what had followed me on platform 4 and I didn't care – I just went.

It is only fair to mention that platform 4 is on "stilts", but it was no echo, as the footsteps continued long after I had stopped moving.

During the following week I asked my opposite leading porter, John Fitch, if he had heard or seen anything on late turn, and he told me that he had also heard footsteps on occasions.

I later transferred to Kenley station and John went to work for National Carriers. I can assure you that every word of my story is absolutely true.'

45
Hibaldstow Crossing

Some signal boxes and crossing keeper's cabins are, by virtue of their locations, very lonely and sometimes very frightening places. These structures are usually warm in winter and cool in summer, but on a wild winter's night when the gales are blowing, the creaks and the movement and the many mysterious noises of the night can make the occupants feel rather ill at ease and wonder if they are really alone. . .

Picture then the lonely gate keeper's cabin situated just by the A15 road in North Lincolnshire near Brigg. Hibaldstow Crossing was the name of the location; the cabin and a small house were the only signs of life.

The crossing keeper's cabin was a little wooden hut close by the railway line, and the gates across the road were of course hand-operated. Indicators in the cabin repeated the instruments in the nearest signal box, letting the crossing keeper know that a train was on the way. The little cabin was rather basic; besides the indicators there was a small coke stove, which gave some warmth, but with the door open so often the heat was quickly lost.

In the mid-1920s a fatal accident occurred at Hibaldstow. One day the crossing keeper (who lived at the Crossing Cottage) was suddenly taken ill and was thus unable to perform his duties. A porter named Kirkman who worked at Scawby & Hibaldstow station was therefore sent to cover the duty at the remote crossing, but subsequent events were to reveal the folly of sending an inexperienced man to do this job, and the man's apparent ignorance of the finer points of the operation was to cost him his life.

As one particular train approached, Mr Kirkman received the information on the cabin indicator and was struggling to open one of the gates, having successfully managed to open the other, when he was run down and killed. The subsequent inquest duly returned a verdict of accidental death, and the whole unfortunate incident was deemed to be closed. Operations returned to normal, but with extra emphasis on safety.

However, later events suggest that poor Mr Kirkman returned to the scene of the accident, because crossing keepers spoke of hearing footsteps near the cabin. Investigations revealed nothing, but my contributor, Mr G. Coverdale, who now lives in Scunthorpe and who worked as crossing keeper at Hibaldstow Crossing, heard the sounds of the footsteps on several occasions and will vouch for the truth of the stories.

Mr Coverdale was very puzzled and frightened at the time, and at first put it down to anything but a paranormal experience, but after several occurrences he began to believe that there was a ghost. No shape was ever seen, but the solid-sounding footsteps approaching the cabin were enough to frighten some of Mr Coverdale's workmates, who were certainly not keen on working the night shift. When anyone heard the strange noises, they would automatically search the area immediately around the cabin for the cause, but none was evident; the supernatural was at work in all its mystery. To find that it was all a practical joke would have been a welcome relief, but no such hoax was discovered to explain the sounds in the middle of the night.

Other night shift staff give slightly varying accounts of their experiences, but they all insist on having heard footsteps and can offer no explanation for them. They all looked round outside the cabin without any result; there was never anyone there.

With the installation of automatic barriers in 1966 the crossing became unmanned. Gone was the gateman and the little old cabin; gone too were the unexplained sounds of the phantom footsteps, for there were no gatemen to feel the hair rise on the backs of their necks as the measured tread approached the cabin.

But people still remember the lonely crossing keeper crouched in the little cabin waiting for the sound of the indicator to warn him of an approaching train, and they remember the dreaded sound of the footsteps and the howling of the wind across the winter landscape.

46
The ghost of Fair Becca

*T*his terrifying experience witnessed by an unsuspecting teenager has been passed on to me by Mr P. Briggs of Bradford. The location for this strange and bizarre event was the Horton branch line of the Great Northern Railway; this no longer exists but it ran from Keighley to Queensbury, where it was joined by the line from Halifax as it descended to Clayton, Great Horton, Horton Park and St Dunstans, terminating at Bradford Exchange.

The story is as follows. A young man who lived in the village of Clayton and worked in one of the textile mills at Great Horton used to travel on the railway to work and back when he could afford it. At other times he had to walk, for pay in those days was not a lot and he had to be careful. On Fridays he received his week's pay so he could buy himself fish and chips at teatime, and he would then perhaps go on to one of the local picture houses, maybe the Plaza, the Grange or the Elysian, after which he would catch the train home. In the 1940s the only other form of transport in the Bradford area was the trams.

One icy winter's night at Great Horton, when the moon lit up the landscape with its translucent glow, the young man waited for the two-coach train to arrive. He was cold and stamped his feet to try and keep warm. Eventually the train came into view; a tank engine was the motive power, running bunker first, and the young man noticed that there were very few passengers on board.

He got on to the train and quickly found an empty

compartment. In a few minutes the guard gave the 'right away', the engine whistled and the train steamed slowly out of the station.

The windows of the compartment were shrouded in vapour as the engine worked hard on the incline towards Clayton. Just beyond Great Horton station the line ran through a cutting; midway along was a bridge carrying Old Corn Lane, and at the end was a footbridge. As the train passed through the cutting the compartment suddenly went icy cold and the steam from the engine cleared, revealing a woman's face pressed against the window pane. The sounds of the train seemed to die away, but the ghastly twisted face of the woman was still pressed to the window. It was horrible – it was as if she was trying to get into the train.

For what seemed an age the young man cowered in the corner of his seat frozen with terror, his eyes wide open with the shock. Then, as suddenly as the face had appeared, it vanished. The sounds of the train's movement came back and it steamed into Clayton station. The young man staggered out of the train, his face ashen, and almost collapsed into the arms of the guard. He blurted out his story and the guard nodded sympathetically. He'd heard it all before – the young man had seen the ghost of Fair Becca.

It seems that Becca was having an affair with another man, but her husband found out and killed her, then threw her body down a well near Brackenhill Park; her ghost is said to haunt the area along the railway line. Apparently her spectre is well known and has been seen on many occasions in recent years. So if anyone fancies seeing it they should trace the old trackbed of the line around dusk or late at night when the moon is full and the owls call 'Beware of Fair Becca'.

47
Strange happenings at Webb House

I have often been asked awkward questions about my collection of railway ghost stories, the main one being 'How do you explain it?' People will always try to find a logical explanation!

The answer is of course that there is no explanation for a supernatural event. People have been probing the intricacies of the paranormal for hundreds of years without any acceptable conclusions. It is simply that some people are able to experience paranormal events, while others are totally unable to do so. So we have the believer and the non-believer, the convictions of each as strong as the experiences themselves.

I met such differing views when I tried to investigate the strange happenings at Webb House in Victoria Avenue, Crewe. Francis William Webb was Chief Mechanical Engineer of the London & North Western Railway from 1871 to 1903. Webb House, which was named after him, was at one time an orphanage for the children of railwaymen, and is now a training school for railway staff.

I received a letter from a Mr H. C. Johnston of Liverpool suggesting that I investigate the alleged happenings in this old building. Seeking further information I wrote to British Rail at Webb House asking for any details that might substantiate the stories I had been told. Their reply was disappointing: they denied that anything untoward had ever happened, just as an unbeliever would. After all, we do not all have the opportunity of seeing signs of the other world, and the writer was frank and sensible. That's it, I thought – end of story.

However, about six months later, to my surprise, I received a letter from a Mrs Fox, wife of the caretaker who looked after Webb House. The Fox family lived in a cottage in the grounds and had several very mystifying experiences both in Webb House and the cottage.

Mrs Fox had apparently read in the local newspaper my letter asking for further material for my railway ghosts book, and her story turned out to be very mystifying, providing plenty of details of her family's experiences in and around Webb House.

Mrs Fox described herself as a practising Christian, feet firmly on the ground and sensible. Her story unfolded as follows:

'Many years ago, during one particularly cold Saturday evening, my family, comprising husband, young son and two little girls, were watching television in our sitting room at Webb Cottage. I was preparing the evening meal and because the cottage was so cold I decided to let them eat in front of the television and enjoy the warmth of the fire. I had carried the cutlery and plates into the room and was returning through the dining room with a tray containing the children's food. As I passed the fireplace I stepped over the extended paws of a large black dog that was lying in front of the fire. When I entered our sitting room I was surprised to find our own Great Dane bitch, Lisa, lying with our younger daughter in front of the fire. Lisa was a brindle colour, definitely not black.

My husband, seeing my startled expression, asked me what was the matter. I hurriedly gave him the tray and shot back into the dining room, but the large black dog had gone! Since then I have seen the black dog only twice in 16 years, but both occasions have left an impression. He is a happy dog; my husband has also seen him and corroborates my experience.

At weekends my husband goes into the main building of Webb House to check that there have been no break-ins or intruders, and in the winter no burst pipes. In the winter months I usually go with him and on one occasion we both heard the sound of a child crying. The cries, very distinct, seemed to be those of a young girl and appeared to be coming from the attic suite. We went up there to investigate, but there was no sign of a child; we had a good look round, expecting to find signs of a break-in (you know what kids are), but nothing was found to explain the sounds. My husband was annoyed – he didn't like mysteries!

We were to hear the sounds on many other occasions, but after thorough searches nothing was ever found. My husband, to his chagrin and worry, has also seen the figure of a well-built gentleman, dressed in a dark suit with either knickerbockers or breeches, long hair, a beard and a vague white cravat. This figure has also been seen several times by various other people.'

Mrs Fox emphasised that she was recalling accurately the experiences of herself and her husband. She strenuously maintained that the truth had been uppermost at all times and that neither she nor her husband were actually frightened or disturbed by the events, although they accepted that there would appear to be no logical explanation for the strange happenings at Webb House. Another example of the veil being lifted to reveal the past. . .?

48
My old friend

*T*his story is taken from *Weekend* magazine of 4-10 April
1979.

My friend Bernie Marks was tall, dark and handsome. He came
from a wealthy family and he had a remarkable capacity for
drink, mostly spirits, which I shared in those days before the war.

Bernie had a Mercedes-Benz motor car and it seemed that the
more he drank the better he drove. Never having seen him quite
sober, I used to wonder if he could manage to drive a car without
a drink inside him. We lived in Manchester in those far-off days
and enjoyed our evenings out together until I got married and
gave up running around with the boys. I settled down to a quiet
family life, just as a married man should, but I heard that Bernie
was still continuing his high life, a real 'good-time boy'.

When the war started Bernie joined up, even though he could
have been exempted as the managing director of a firm working
on government contracts. As it was, he found himself driving
important officers round London. I wondered about his drinking
and driving.

Because of a First World War wound I was exempt and had a
job as a manager of a clothing factory, plus my Civil Defence
duties. By 1945 I had three children and my boss offered an all-
expenses-paid holiday for them and my wife as a bonus for my
hard work.

They duly set off to the best hotel in Blackpool for a fortnight
and I was allowed two long weekends with them. One Monday

morning I caught the early train from Blackpool to Manchester to get back to work. As we approached Manchester's Victoria station another train pulled alongside. I was sitting by the window and suddenly I saw my old friend Bernie Marks in the train opposite. I was astonished because he looked so pale and ill and his eyes were staring out of the window into space, but there was no doubt that it was Bernie.

I let my window down and waved to him as our trains moved side by side. By now we were quite close and I shouted his name as loud as I could, but he just stared blankly into space, seemingly oblivious of my frantic efforts to attract his attention.

Bernie's train eventually diverged and I said to a passenger in my compartment, 'That's my oldest friend I was waving to.'

To my surprise the other replied, 'I didn't see anyone.'

I said, 'Well I'll catch up with him at Victoria station.'

'No you won't,' said my companion. 'That train is going into Manchester Central.'

He was right, so I went on to the office intending to ring Bernie's home as soon as possible to arrange to meet up again, but pressure of work prevented my making the call.

It was not until the Friday that I decided to go to the old pub where Bernie drank, thinking he might be there. Instead his brother was there.

'How's Bernie?' I asked him.

'Don't you know?' he said. 'Bernie's dead – he was killed in a car crash last week in London.'

I was stunned. I heard Bernie's brother say, 'They brought his body back by train and we met the coffin at Central station last Monday morning.'

With a chill I realised that I must have seen my old friend's ghost peering from the window of the train carrying his body home. So he *was* in the train after all and only I could see him.

I didn't believe in ghosts then and I still have my doubts, but I shall always believe in what I saw that morning.

There is a curious postscript to the story. The autopsy on Bernie showed that there was no alcohol in his body. It gave me a wry smile. I always knew Bernie could not drive well without a drink.

49

The return of Binns Bankcroft

A few years ago a railway enthusiast volunteer, whom we will call Paul Smith, journeyed to Haworth on the preserved Keighley & Worth Valley Railway. He was keen to play his part in the restoration of trains and the gradual bringing back to life of the pleasant 5-mile-long branch line. He lived in Lincolnshire and found it difficult to get over to Yorkshire very often, but the trip was always worth the trouble; the interesting work of reclaiming the past and the challenge of operating the line as a tourist attraction spurred him on.

Some of the volunteers who came from afar were accommodated in a sleeping coach in the goods yard at Haworth. From there they had a good view of the stone-walled yard and the adjacent road, although sometimes the view would be blocked by rolling-stock stored in the yard; soon a new multi-purpose shed was to be built on the yard to remedy lack of covered space.

One summer night, after chatting to his mates about the day's events, Paul decided to have a walk round the yard before turning in. The night was warm and almost windless, the paraphernalia of railway equipment occupied the many corners of the yard, and shadows were everywhere. Paul was pleasantly tired and content. He was not aware of anything untoward until he caught a glimpse of something moving in a corner of the yard. Puzzled, he approached the area and was able to make out the hazy shape of an wizened old man holding a long pole. The figure seemed solid enough, but the haze made it difficult to discern the features.

Paul froze to the spot, fascinated by the scene. The area where the man stood seemed to show other features as if with a different background; part of the scene had altered. Paul felt compelled to play the part of observer, and as the figure moved about, waving the long pole and gesturing, he started to move forward to get a better look at him, but as he approached the man seemed to melt away.

Paul ran back to the sleeping coach, but the sound of snoring told him that most of the inhabitants were asleep, so he got into his bunk and lay awake, turning over in his mind what he had seen in the yard. He was not frightened, more baffled. He certainly was not psychic, and dismissed the idea of ghosts. Sleep claimed him at last.

In the morning he could not wait to discuss the mystery with his mates. A good laugh was had by all, although this response did not help his attempts to find a logical explanation for his experience, and he was unable to get the matter out of his mind all day.

A few days later he found himself talking to an old hand whose father had worked for British Railways at Haworth many years before. Paul mentioned his experience to him and he did not seem at all surprised.

'It would be old Bankcroft you saw; he sometimes appears to have a look round,' he said.

Paul nodded. 'I've heard of him in the last few days, but I thought it was some kind of joke.'

The other shook his head. 'Oh no, Binns Bankcroft thinks he still works in this yard.'

It appears that Bankcroft was a coal merchant in Haworth in the latter part of the last century. His premises were located in the goods yard across the road from the railway station so he did not have far to go to pick up his coal supply. When the coal was shunted into the yard Binns was always there to help, his shunting pole in his hand, and when the wagons had discharged their load, he would drive his horse and cart into the yard and load up for his local deliveries. He liked to be in the yard when the coal train arrived, and he would try to direct operations for shunting the wagons, bawling instructions to the engine driver and guard. They regarded him as a damned nuisance who did nothing but get in the way, causing them many anxious moments as he darted in and out between the wagons. They feared for his safety, but he was always there and they could do nothing to keep him away from the station.

One winter's day in 1882 Binns was supervising operations as usual as the coal wagons were shunted into Haworth goods yard. He was waving his pole and bellowing instructions to the guard who was trying to understand his shouts in the high wind. Binns was a little hard of hearing so his replies to the driver and guard were also made difficult to comprehend – it was therefore not surprising that problems would occur. Binns was moving in and around the wagons when, failing to heed the warning shouts of the guard, he was caught between two vehicles and the life was crushed out of him. The subsequent inquest held at the nearby Royal Oak Inn returned a verdict of 'Death by Misadventure', so that was the end of Binns Bankcroft . . . or was it?

In 1968 Haworth goods yard became the scene of much activity when the Keighley & Worth Valley Preservation Society began operations to re-open the line. The goods shed was found to be very useful for repairs and attention to locomotives, while the yard with its sidings was invaluable for storing stock of all kinds.

Paul was not the only preservation volunteer to encounter Mr Bankcroft. One night a man who was visiting the railway saw a light on in the goods shed. Thinking that it was rare for anyone to be working so late, he went to investigate; perhaps someone had inadvertently left the light on. As he entered the old building everything was quiet and very still. The strange light seemed to be coming from the corner . . . a soft light, almost as if it were an oil lamp. Suddenly the figure of a man emerged and walked towards him, a pole in his hand. Our friend was frozen to the spot and then, as suddenly as it had appeared, the figure melted in front of his astonished eyes.

To this day various people swear that they have seen the ghost of Binns, and other people vouch for unexplained happenings in and around the goods shed. A lot of leg-pulling goes on regarding the sightings, but many are unshakeable in their belief that they have seen the shadow of the old man, and heard his footsteps in the yard.